Internalizing *the* Faith

A Pilgrim's Catechism

J. Brandon Burks

Fontes Press

Internalizing the Faith:
A Pilgrim's Catechism

Copyright © 2018 by J. Brandon Burks

ISBN: 1-948048-03-5

ISBN-13: 978-1-948048-03-3

Scripture quotations are from the ESV® Bible (The Holy Bible, English Standard Version®), copyright © 2001 by Crossway, a publishing ministry of Good News Publishers. Used by permission. All rights reserved.

All rights reserved. No part of this publication may be reproduced, stored in a retrieval system, or transmitted in any form or by any means—electronic, mechanical, photocopy, recording, or any other—except for brief quotations in printed reviews, without the prior permission of the publisher.

Fontes Press
www.fontespress.com

"Brandon Burks has produced a valuable catechism. It is filled with concise, coherent, biblically grounded, theologically sound answers to important pertinent questions. Without laboring under jargon, the answers introduce the student to sophisticated and vital theological ideas such as active and passive obedience, the covenants, election, reprobation, some hermeneutical issues, and striking principles of ethics. Every parent and every pastor should be pleased to have this valuable resource available for their calling to instruct in truth those under their care."

Dr. Thomas J. Nettles
Professor of Church History, retired
The Southern Baptist Theological Seminary

"Brandon Burks has composed a fine, insightful catechism. In several questions he addresses issues of contemporary importance that composers of older catechisms may have been unable to anticipate. A person who memorizes this catechism will have a good foundation for a lifetime of growth in the Christian life."

Dr. Jim Scott Orrick
Professor of Literature and Culture
Boyce College

"I love *Internalizing the Faith* because I love it when complex, theological concepts are presented with precision and clarity. But, there is another reason I love this catechism: I love the uniqueness of how each of its three sections begin with the doctrine of God and how each section ends with practical application. It is like having three catechisms in one. I haven't seen anything quite like this. Questions regarding God, the law, Christ, salvation, and the church are contained in each section. This is ingenious because it pedagogically corresponds with the way students learn. Rather than answering every major question about the doctrine of God before transitioning to the other major doctrines of Scriptures, Brandon provides the student with a basic overview of all the major doctrines in Part 1, and then revisits those doctrines by diving deeper in Part 2, and again even deeper in Part 3. This makes it a wonderful teaching tool for all. I highly recommend *Internalizing the Faith* and the teaching it contains to both students and teachers alike."

Dr. Jeffery D. Johnson
Author of *The Kingdom of God*, *The Absurdity of Unbelief*, and *The Pursuit of Glory*
Pastor of Grace Bible Church, AR

"The best catechisms are not written by theologians, but by theologians who are fathers; Brandon Burks is both and gave us a catechism that is quite remarkable for its usefulness and uniqueness. The introduction provides a good biblical and historical background on the use of catechisms to internalize the faith. The catechism itself is filled with the rich doctrine of the Christian Church presented in a very pedagogical fashion with some important applications for the Christian life. The end notes associated with each question give additional biblical support and essential bibliographical resources for further study. This catechism will definitely instruct and serve the budding theologian as well as the mature one. I highly recommend it!"

Pascal Denault
Author of *The Distinctiveness of Baptist Covenant Theology*
Pastor of Église réformée baptiste of St-Jérôme, QC

DEDICATION

To my loving wife, Traci, and to my children,
evidence of God's bounty:
May the truths in this catechism endure in
your minds, penetrate your hearts, and
manifest in your lives.

> O God, attend me in every part of my arduous and trying pilgrimage; I need the same counsel, defense, comfort I found at my beginning. Let my religion be more obvious to my conscience, more perceptible to those around. While Jesus is representing me in heaven, may I reflect him on earth, while he pleads my cause, may I show forth his praise.
> – Valley of Vision[2]

I thank the youth at Crossroads Community Church in Upper Darby, PA. Without the experience of drilling you with catechisms, this current work would not have been written. Truly, you have taught me much.

Dr. Fred Nelson has been a blessing to this project. He worked through early manuscripts, making recommendations and pressing me to simplify at every point. The presentation of this work was greatly enhanced by his time and care. Thank you for sacrificing your time for this project, and, even more, thank you for your friendship!

Having read this catechism with a view toward the effectiveness of its pedagogy, one of my former

---

[2] Arthur Bennett, ed., "God Enjoyed," in *Valley of Vison: A Collection of Puritan Prayers and Devotions* (1975; repr., Carlisle, PA: The Banner of Truth, 2015), 19.

AUTHOR'S PREFACE

Fathers... bring [your children] up in the discipline and instruction of the Lord.
– Ephesians 6:4

The proper study of God's elect is God; the proper study of a Christian is the Godhead. The highest science, the loftiest speculation, the mightiest philosophy, which can ever engage the attention of a child of God, is the name, the nature, the person, the work, the doings, and the existence of the great God whom he calls Father.
– C. H. Spurgeon[1]

---

[1] Quoted in J. I. Packer, *Knowing God* (Downer Groves, IL: IVP Books, 1973), 17.

catechumen, Benjamin Doctor, has provided a much-needed perspective. Thank you for giving me feedback regarding the catechism's clarity and understandability.

Jason Hudson also has made helpful suggestions. As a professor of English with pastoral experience, his wisdom and command of the English language has proven beneficial to the overall presentation of this catechism. Thank you, friend!

I would also like to thank Traci Burks, Jocelyn Groff, Matthew Gay, Jonathan Brack, Jim Burks, Sharon Burks, and Michael Caligaris for proofreading earlier manuscripts. The feedback I received aided the outcome of the catechism, for which I am very grateful.

Finally, I would like to thank Dr. Jeffrey Johnson, Dr. Jim Scott Orrick, and Dr. Thomas Nettles. Their encouragements, insights, and theological acumen have been extremely valuable. Thank you, brothers!

CONTENTS

Author's Preface	xi
Introduction	1
Part 1	19
Part 2	31
Part 3	43
Endnotes	53

INTRODUCTION

God wants His people to know the things He has revealed in His Word (Deut 29:29; Ps 119:11; Mark 12:24) and to be ready to speak those things when called upon (Prov 15:28; 2 Tim 4:2; 1 Pet 3:15). Catechisms are a blessing to Christ's Church, for by them Christians have a readied answer to common questions. Catechisms are both biblical and deeply rooted in Protestant history. The word "catechism" comes from the Greek word *katēkeō* (κατηχέω), meaning "to teach" or "to instruct."[1] Luke wrote Theophilus an orderly

---

[1] Frederick William Danker, ed., *A Greek-English Lexicon of the New Testament and Other Early Christian Literature*, 3rd ed. (Chicago: University of Chicago Press,

account so that he "may have certainty concerning the things [he had] been *taught*" (Luke 1:4), and, elsewhere, he wrote that Apollos had "been *instructed* in the way of the Lord" (Acts 18:25). Paul, likewise, wrote "Let the one who is *taught* the word share all good things with the one who *teaches*" (Gal 6:6).[2]

Scripture gives a clear command to learn and to grow in doctrinal understanding. The writer of Hebrews exhorts his listeners, "Let us leave the elementary doctrine of Christ and go on to maturity" (6:1). What is more, we are called to be "obedient" to the "standard of teaching" to which we are committed (Rom 6:17), to "follow the pattern of sound words" (2 Tim 1:13), to be "devoted" to the apostles' teachings (Acts 2:42), to "stand firm and hold to the traditions" we are taught by the apostles in Scripture (2 Thess 2:15), which is nothing less than the "whole counsel of

---

2000), 534.

[2] For a more thorough treatment of the Bible's use of *katēkeō*, see: J. I. Packer and Gary A. Parrett, *Grounded in the Gospel: Building Believers the Old-Fashioned Way* (Grand Rapids, MI: Baker, 2010), 33-50.

Introduction

God" (Acts 20:27).[3]

God's revelation in Scripture belongs "to us and to our children forever" (Deut 29:29), and, therefore, we must be diligent to teach the next generation, using every opportunity to do so (Deut 11:19). Without a doubt, the following verse is one of the more concerning in Scripture: "And all that generation also were gathered to their fathers. And there arose another generation after them who did not know the LORD or the work that he had done for Israel" (Judg 2:10). Here we see a chilling reality: knowledge of the faith can be lost in a single generation. Catechizing is a method of teaching "the faith that was once for all delivered to the saints" (Jude 1:3), so as to preserve the content of the Christian faith for generations to come.

Catechisms were a key tool for teaching the faith during and after the Reformation. Martin Luther was serious about catechizing, even recommending that those who refused catechetical instruction be barred from the

---

[3] John Piper, "A Baptist Catechism," *Desiring God*, January 1, 1986 (accessed June 14, 2017), http://www.desiringgod.org/articles/a-baptist-catechism.

sacraments and denied food.[4] While a bit extreme, Luther's standard illustrates the vital role catechizing played during the Reformation. John Calvin, a second generation Reformer, warned, "[T]he Church of God will never preserve itself without a Catechism, for it is like the seed to keep the good grain from dying out and using it to multiply from age to age."[5] Puritan Thomas Watson similarly wrote, "To preach and not to catechise is to build without a foundation."[6] J. I. Packer further elaborates on catechesis in the Reformation and post-Reformation periods:

> In the sixteenth and seventeenth centuries all Protestant church leaders were agreed that catechizing from childhood through adulthood was an *essential element in church life*, without which the church could hardly survive, or hope to survive....The Prayer Book of

---

[4] Carl R. Trueman, *Luther on the Christian Life: Cross and Freedom* (Wheaton, IL: Crossway, 2015), 112n31.

[5] John Calvin, *Selected Works of John Calvin*, 7 vols., ed. Henry Beveridge and Jules Bonnet (Grand Rapids, MI: Baker Book House, 1983), 5:191, brackets added.

[6] As quoted in: Thomas J. Nettles and Steve Weaver, *Teaching Truth, Training Hearts: The Study of Catechisms in Baptist Life,* rev. ed. (Cape Coral, FL: Founders Press, 2017), 32.

INTRODUCTION

> the Church of England had in it a children's catechism that clergy, along with parents and godparents, were required to teach, and the children were required to learn before being confirmed and entering into the Church's communicant life.... For faith, to the Puritans, started with factual knowledge—knowledge of who and what God is, who and what Jesus Christ is, and what the gospel is—and *the purpose of catechizing was to open the door to the life of faith by laying faith's cognitive foundations.*[7]

The catechisms drafted during and after the Reformation were seen not as Scripture's equal, but as subordinate summaries of Scripture's content. Only Scripture is the "norming norm," which means a catechism can only be the "normed norm," always subject to the correction of Scripture.[8] But as a normed summary of the Christian faith, our families and churches can rely on catechisms for instructing both the young and old, while preserving the faith for generations to

---

[7] J. I. Packer, *Puritan Portraits* (Fearn, Ross-shire: Christian Focus, 2012), 16, emphasis added.

[8] Carl R. Trueman, *The Creedal Imperative* (Wheaton, IL: Crossway, 2012), 80.

come.[9]

Unfortunately, catechizing has fallen on hard times in contemporary evangelicalism. Where catechizing was once seen as a spiritual lifeline, it is now seen as outdated and irrelevant. Church historian and theologian Thomas Nettles laments, "Life at the beginning of the third millennium A.D. pulsates witticisms, opinions, and even reasons that would assign a book on catechisms to the dust bin of antiquarian irrelevancies."[10] Sharing this same sober awareness, theologians J. I. Packer and Gary A. Parrett confess, "We are well aware that in advocating a renewal of catechesis we fight an uphill battle and swim against the stream."[11] Nevertheless, it must be done, for,

> Superficial smatterings of truth, blurry notions about God and godliness, and thoughtlessness about issues of living—careerwise, communitywise, familywise, and churchwise—are all too often the marks of evangelical congregations today.... We think that as long as catechesis, which was the strength of Christian

---

[9] Trueman expounds upon ways in which a catechism can function in the life of the church. See ibid., 153-154.

[10] Nettles and Weaver, *Teaching Truth, Training Hearts*, 9.

[11] Packer and Parrett, *Grounded in the Gospel*, 10.

Introduction

nurture in the past, continues to be out of fashion, these shortcomings are not likely to disappear."[12]

Why We Should Catechize

If we desire to grow in the knowledge of God and to pass on "the whole counsel of God" to the next generation, we must be diligent to catechize.[13] Indeed, not doing so will leave this

---

[12] Ibid., 16-17. Packer and Parrett go on to advocate for trained catechists to work alongside Bible study leaders and Sunday school teachers in the church: "It is our belief that in today's congregations there is a need to give the same sort of training to a new generation of catechists that we now give to Bible study group leaders and Sunday school teachers. Catechists are teachers whose special task is to ground worshipers of every age in the truths Christians live by and in the ways Christians are to live by those truths. Why is this necessary? Because all congregants, adults no less than the young, need a full initial grounding in these things, followed by regular revisiting and deepened exploration of them" (ibid., 17).

[13] Cornelius Van Til, an example for us all, noted that the catechetical teaching load for his church far exceeded the teaching load for his seminary class. Muether comments, "Van Til placed great stress on catechetical instruction in his pastorate. So strong was his preparation for catechism classes that when he reflected on it later, he

and the successive generations unmoored, unable to weather the spiritual and theological storms on the horizon. Punctilious to catechize his own church, Charles Haddon Spurgeon wrote:

> In matters of doctrine you will find orthodox congregations frequently changed to heterodoxy in the course of thirty or forty years, and that is because, too often there has been no catechising of the children in the essential doctrines of the Gospel. For my part, I am more and more persuaded that the study of a good Scriptural catechism is of infinite value to our children.[14]

Doubtless, the false dichotomies of believing versus belonging, knowing versus feeling, or head versus heart have only helped push catechisms out of our churches, allowing mysticism and secularism to infiltrate our families and our pews.[15] Critics may say that Christianity is not a list

---

computed that his catechetical teaching load at Spring Lake far exceeded his Westminster teaching load." John R. Muether, *Cornelius Van Til: Reformed Apologist and Churchman* (Phillipsburg, NJ: P&R, 2008), 58.

[14] Quoted in Nettles and Weaver, *Teaching Truth, Training Hearts,* 119.

[15] For more on the believing versus belonging

of doctrines but is, rather, a vital relationship. Some maintain that to *know* God is experiential and *not* doctrinal. To be sure, there is a necessary relational aspect in knowing God. John wrote: "And this is eternal life, that they know you, the only true God, and Jesus Christ whom you have sent" (John 17:3). This knowledge, says Andreas Köstenberger, "does not refer merely to cognitive knowledge (the Greek conception); it means living in fellowship with God."[16] But it is pure mysticism to assert that we *know* God better by *not* knowing Him intellectually, for mysticism praises and promotes "a *total lack* of understanding and of thinking. It prizes the ineffable above all and sees reason and thinking as obstacles to true faith."[17] Biblical faith, by contrast, is content-laden. Scott Oliphint remarks, "Theology is to be God-centered; it comes from Him, it should teach us

---

dichotomy, see: Carl R. Trueman, *The Real Scandal of the Evangelical Mind* (Chicago, IL: Moody, 2011).

[16] Andreas Köstenberger, *John*, Baker Exegetical Commentary on the New Testament (Grand Rapids, MI: Baker Academic, 2004), 488.

[17] K. Scott Oliphint, *The Majesty of Mystery: Celebrating the Glory of an Incomprehensible God* (Bellingham, WA: Lexham Press, 2016), 8; cf. 9-10.

more and more about Him, and that teaching should lead us inexorably to praise Him.... Worship is not simply a context; it is a *response*, meant to flow from our understanding of God."[18]

Knowing God requires *both* doctrinal knowledge and relational knowledge. How can you have fellowship if you do not know the person with whom you are in fellowship? Having said this, doctrinal knowledge is no guarantee that a person is in fellowship with God. Like the devil, one can know true facts about God and be hell-bound (cf. James 2:19). In his classic work, *Knowing God*, J. I. Packer writes, "There can be no spiritual health without doctrinal knowledge; but it is equally true that there can be no spiritual health *with* it, if it is sought for the wrong purposes and valued by the wrong standard."[19] Packer bids us to look to the Psalmist who "was interested in truth and orthodoxy, in biblical teaching and theology, not as ends in themselves, but as means to further ends of life and godliness. His ultimate concern was with the knowledge and service of the great God whose truth he sought to

---

[18] Ibid., 21.
[19] Packer, *Knowing God*, 22.

INTRODUCTION

understand."[20]

My hope is that the knowledge gained through this catechism will lead to greater fellowship with and worship of the God we love. In fact, memorizing a catechism can be one of the ways in which we love God with all our minds (Mark 12:30). Oliphint explains:

> But what does it mean to love God with our minds? At minimum, this means that we are to know God—that is, we are to read and understand what Scripture says about God, and to submit intellectually (and otherwise) to that teaching. *We are to think God's thoughts after Him.* Those thoughts are found in God's revelation. When we read Scripture, when we study it, we are to see it as the only true description of what reality is like. We are to reorient our thinking, so that the things around us, and within us, take on the truth that God has spoken.[21]

---

[20] Ibid., 22-23; cf. Pss 119:1-2, 5, 12, 18, 97, 103, 125.

[21] Oliphint, *The Majesty of Mystery,* 12; emphasis added.

Internalizing the Faith

How to Use This Catechism

On becoming a father, I was burdened to write a catechism that would serve my children in their Christian pilgrimages. As our culture and contexts change, so too do the spiritual challenges. My children were at the forefront of my mind as I wrote this catechism, doing my best to anticipate the sins that will tempt them, the cultural and political features that will challenge them, the heresies and false doctrines that will confront them, and the demonic oppositions that will test them.

In this catechism, I endeavored to maintain simplicity combined with terse precision. Some features include the use of personal pronouns to promote ownership of the truth. In each, a Scripture citation is listed at the end of the answer for the purpose of being memorized with the answer.[22] In the endnotes, I include additional

---

[22] The purpose is to memorize the citation but not necessarily the entire verse. So, for example, the catechumen would say, "John 3:16," rather than reciting the entire verse. By having at least one Scripture citation memorized, the catechumen will have a starting place

Introduction

Scripture references and other recommended reading to further explore each answer.[23] Uniquely, this catechism addresses practical life issues such as anxiety, money, marriage, addiction, and temptation.

What is more, this catechism is ordered pedagogically, in the order in which it is to be memorized. Providing a helpful scope and sequence, I divided the catechism into three parts: questions 1-40, questions 41-76, and questions 77-107. Part one includes basic truths about Scripture, Christ, the Ten Commandments, faith, and repentance. Building upon this, part two includes questions on the Trinity, the law, salvation, and the ordinances. Finally, part three includes questions on the image of God, the covenants, and union with Christ.

Each part has the same basic flow as the other parts. This allows the catechumen to survey the basics of each of the theological topics (or *loci*) in

---

when scripturally defending or explaining one the catechetical answers.

[23] The books listed in the endnotes were used in forming the answer and/or are recommended for further exploration. The recommended readings are listed with the simpler or more central book first.

part one, only to comb over the same *loci* in subsequent parts, gaining depth and precision. The following chart illustrates this:

Part 1	Part 2	Part 3
Bible/God	God	God
Sin/Law	Law	Law/Covenants
Jesus Christ	Jesus Christ	Jesus Christ
Salvation	Salvation	Salvation
Mankind	Mankind	Mankind/Angels
Church	Church	Church
Application	Application	Application

In explaining Luther's catechetical method, Carl Trueman wrote, "The order is to teach the form of sound words first, and then to teach the people what these words mean."[24] While younger students might not understand aspects of what they are memorizing, in the words of Miss Ophelia from the American novel *Uncle Tom's Cabin*, "after they are grown up, it'll come to them."[25] The

---

[24] Trueman, *Luther on the Christian Life*, 112.

[25] Harriet Beecher Stowe, *Uncle Tom's Cabin*, ed. by Mary R. Reichardt, Ignatius Critical Edition (San Francisco: Ignatius Press, 2009), 326-327

INTRODUCTION

student is to memorize the exact words, because, as they are nurtured in the church, they will mature in their understanding of what those words convey.[26]

Consider what it might look like for parents to use this catechism with their children. I began catechizing my son when he was four years old and just starting to learn to read. In order to put the catechism into his memory, I had a five-step process that I would repeat every day until that particular catechism question was committed to memory. After first reading a catechism question and answer aloud, my son would then repeat after me, walking through the answer a segment at a time. Once he had repeated the answer twice, I would then explain the answer to him one concept at a time. In other words, I would

---

[26] Spurgeon said, "Even if the youngsters do not understand all the questions and answers... yet, abiding in their memories, it will be infinite service when the time of understanding comes, to have known these very excellent, wise, and judicious definitions of the things of God... It will be a blessing to them—the greatest of all blessing... a blessing in life and death, in time and eternity, the best of blessings God Himself can give." As quoted in: Nettles and Weaver, *Teaching Truth, Training Hearts,* 119.

summarize the teaching and explain some of the more difficult words. After this, he would repeat after me once more, walking through the answer a segment at a time. By this time, my four-year-old was usually squirmy and ready for something else. As he played with a toy, I would recite the catechism aloud five more times in a row.

For children who are able to read, I would write out the catechism on a chalkboard. We would begin by reading it aloud together. I would then erase one of the words on the chalkboard. We would recite it aloud again, testing to see if we remembered the word that was erased. I would then erase another word, and on we would continue until the board was completely blank and we were able to recite that particular catechism question and answer from memory.

Catechizing can be a difficult task. It requires endurance and a great deal of love to instill these words and these truths into a catechumen's mind and heart. With young children or stubborn learners, the task only becomes more tedious. Yet, we must press on with joy and love, diligence and perseverance. When we become weary or discouraged, St. Augustine encourages us to "bear in mind out of what death of error the man is passing over

INTRODUCTION

into the life of faith."[27] Even when, perhaps, the monotony seems burdensome to us, or we grow tired of combing over the same basic doctrines again and again, it should bring great joy to us to know that we are, as Augustine says, "leading a miserable soul... through the path of peace."[28]

While I hope parents find this catechism useful for their children, I also created it for the seasoned Christian. Even as a doctor of theology and a preacher, Luther wrote, "I must still read and study daily, and yet I cannot master it as I wish, but must remain a child and pupil of the catechism, and am glad so to remain."[29] No one is too old or too educated to benefit from this catechism.

To the child, the new convert, and the life-long Christian, I pray you dig deeply into this catechism to the glory and praise of Christ and the building up of his church. May *Internalizing The*

---

[27] St. Augustine, *On The Catechising of the Uninstructed*, trans. by S. D. F. Salmond (Philadelphia, PA: Dalcasssian, 2017), 21-22.

[28] Ibid.

[29] Martin Luther, "The Larger Catechism," *The Book of Concord: The Confessions of the Lutheran Church* (accessed June 14, 2017), http://bookofconcord.org/lc-1-intro.php.

INTERNALIZING THE FAITH

Faith: A Pilgrim's Catechism arm the coming generations to meet the spiritual and theological battles they will face. May the Holy Spirit use the truths contained herein to seal Christ upon your heart as you behold his beauty and lordship.

PART 1

On the Bible and God

Q.1 *What is the Bible?*
A. The Bible is God's written Word in a unified and sufficient collection of sixty-six books that focus on Jesus Christ, each book being authoritative, clear in its central message, without the possibility of error, and self-authenticating. **2 Timothy 3:15-17.**[1]

Q.2 *How was God's Word written?*
A. God's word was written by human authors as the Holy Spirit carried them along, so that every word written was breathed out by God. **2 Peter 1:20-21.**[2]

Q.3 *Who is God?*
A. God is spirit, infinite, eternal, sovereign, love, just, faithful, patient, gracious, merciful, glorious, holy, unchangeable, without parts, all-knowing, all-wise, all-good, all-present, all-powerful, and of Himself. **Exodus 3:14.**[3]

ON SIN AND THE LAW

Q.4 *What was the Fall?*
A. The Fall was the event in which Adam, our representative, rebelled against God by eating the forbidden fruit, whereby all humanity became guilty of Adam's sin, enslaved to sin's power, and separated from God. **Romans 5:12-19.**[4]

Q.5 *What is sin?*
A. Sin is rebellion against God and a disregard for His glory by doing what He forbids or by not doing what He commands. **James 4:17.**[5]

Q.6 *What does the 1st commandment require?*
A. The first commandment requires that I believe and trust only in the Triune God of Scripture. **Exodus 20:3.**[6]

Part 1

Q.7 *What does the 2nd commandment require?*
A. The second commandment requires that I not make images of God but should worship Him according to Scripture alone. **Exodus 20:4-6.**[7]

Q.8 *What does the 3rd commandment require?*
A. The third commandment requires that I not use the name of God in a worthless way, whether in thought, word, or deed. **Exodus 20:7.**[8]

Q.9 *What does the 4th commandment require?*
A. The fourth commandment requires that I spend each Lord's Day longing to enter God's eternal glory by resting from my labor, worshipping God, and serving others. **Exodus 20:8.**[9]

Q.10 *What does the 5th commandment require?*
A. The fifth commandment requires that I honor and obey my parents and authorities as I would the Lord. **Exodus 20:12.**[10]

Q.11 *What does the 6th commandment require?*
A. The sixth commandment requires that I not murder or hate another person, but should promote life and good-will from fertilization to natural death. **Exodus 20:13.**[11]

Internalizing the Faith

Q.12 *What does the 7th commandment require?*
A. The seventh commandment requires that I not commit adultery but remain chaste in thought, word, and deed. **Exodus 20:14.**[12]

Q.13 *What does the 8th commandment require?*
A. The eight commandment requires that I not steal or deal carelessly with that which belongs to another. **Exodus 20:15.**[13]

Q.14 *What does the 9th commandment require?*
A. The ninth commandment requires that I interact honestly with others and keep my tongue from speaking lies. **Exodus 20:16.**[14]

Q.15 *What does the 10th commandment require?*
A. The tenth commandment requires that I not covet anything that belongs to my neighbor but be content with everything God has provided me. **Exodus 20:17.**[15]

PART 1

ON JESUS CHRIST

Q.16 *Who is Jesus?*
A. Jesus is the eternal Son of God, the second Person in the Trinity, who took upon Himself a human nature; and He will forever be fully God and fully man in one person, the only Mediator between God and man. **1 Timothy 2:5.**[16]

Q.17 *What is a type in the Old Testament?*
A. A type in the Old Testament is a person, event, or institution that God ordained to symbolize, to anticipate, and to point to Jesus or the Church as the climactic fulfillment of the type.
Romans 5:14.[17]

Q.18 *What was the Incarnation?*
A. The incarnation was the event in which the eternal Son of God became man, was conceived by the power of the Holy Spirit in the womb of the virgin Mary, and yet was without sin.
Luke 1:31.[18]

Q.19 *What was the purpose of Jesus' earthly life and ministry?*
A. The purpose of Jesus' earthly life and ministry was for Him to vicariously keep the law of God as the last Adam, to fulfill Scripture, to defeat the devil, to instruct sinners on the way to salvation, to inaugurate the new creational kingdom, to be an example to His followers, and to accomplish those things that would lead to His crucifixion and resurrection. **Luke 19:10.**[19]

Q.20 *What was the atonement?*
A. The atonement was the once-for-all act of Jesus on the cross, whereby He propitiated God's wrath against the elect and died as their substitute, thereby expiating their sins. **1 Peter 2:24.**[20]

Q.21 *What was the resurrection?*
A. The resurrection was the act of the Triune God whereby Jesus rose bodily from the grave, conquered death, and became a life-giving spirit. **Acts 2:32-33.**[21]

Part 1

Q.22 *What was the ascension?*
A. The ascension was the act of bringing Jesus to the right hand of God the Father in heaven, from where he would send the Holy Spirit, rule over creation, and intercede on behalf of the saints. **Acts 1:9.**[22]

Q.23 *What will happen when Jesus returns?*
A. When Jesus returns, He will gather His elect from every generation, afflict vengeance upon those who neither know God nor obey His gospel, and bring forth His Kingdom in the New Heavens and the New Earth. **Revelation 19:11-16.**[23]

On Salvation

Q.24 *What is saving faith?*
A. Saving faith is a gift from God whereby, seeing Christ to be our all-satisfying treasure, we rest upon Him alone for our salvation and walk in the obedience of faith. **Ephesians 2:8-9.**[24]

Q.25 *What is repentance?*
A. Repentance is a gift from God that allows us to confess, to turn from, and to hate sin. **Acts 5:31.**[25]

Q.26 *What is the general call of God?*
A. The general call of God is a genuine offer of salvation open to all who hear the gospel. **Matthew 11:25-30.**[26]

Q.27 *What must you do to be saved from the coming judgment?*
A. To be saved from the coming judgment, I must confess that I am a sinner deserving God's wrath and repent of my sins; I must receive Jesus Christ, believing that He took the penalty for my sins on the cross, that He died and rose from the grave; and I must trust in Him alone for my salvation. **Acts 16:30-32.**[27]

Q.28 *Why must you work diligently to endure in the faith?*
A. I must work diligently to endure in the faith lest I abandon Christ, thereby trampling underfoot the Son of God and suffering eternal punishment for my unrighteousness. **Acts 11:23.**[28]

Q.29 *How can a Christian have assurance of salvation?*
A. A Christian can have assurance of salvation by resting in the promises of God for all who believe,

and by the Holy Spirit who gives new birth and manifests fruit in the life of every believer. **Romans 10:9-13.**[29]

On Mankind

Q.30 *What is meant by the broad image of God?*
A. By the broad image of God, it is meant that our whole being, including our bodies, souls, cognition, behavior, emotions, and relational abilities, reflect God, even after the Fall. **Genesis 1:27.**[30]

Q.31 *What is meant by the narrow image of God?*
A. By the narrow image of God, it is meant that we reflect God in true knowledge, righteousness, and holiness; and while lost due to the Fall, it is being renewed for those in Christ. **Ephesians 4:24.**[31]

On the Church

Q.32 *What is the church?*
A. The church, the Bride of Christ, consists of those whom God has called out of spiritual darkness into a biblically governed community to

worship and to grow through the preaching of the Word, the ordinances, and church discipline; and is tasked with making disciples of all nations. **1 Peter 2:9-10.**[32]

Q.33 *What is prayer?*
A. Prayer is thanking, praising, and petitioning God in the name of Christ for things agreeable to His will, in faith and by the Holy Spirit, with confession of our sin. **1 John 5:14.**[33]

Q.34 *What is fasting?*
A. Fasting is abstaining from food or some enjoyment for a period of time for spiritual concerns, focusing on Christ and His purposes in the world. **Matthew 6:16-18.**[34]

APPLICATION

Q.35 *What does it mean to be a pilgrim?*
A. Being a pilgrim means that I am not of this world, for my citizenship is in heaven; and that I am passing through this world as a sojourner on the narrow path to the heavenly city.
Hebrews 11:13-16.[35]

PART 1

Q.36 *What is the purpose of your life?*
A. The purpose of my life is to bring glory to the Triune God, to find Him as the greatest treasure of my heart, and to enjoy Him always as my highest pleasure. **Psalm 16:5-11.**[36]

Q.37 *Why are you not to love the world?*
A. I am not to love the world because if I do, the love of the Father is not in me; for the desires of the world are not from the Father but are passing away with the world. **1 John 2:15-17.**[37]

Q.38 *What does it mean for you to fear God?*
A. To fear God means that I have a reverential fear and awe of God—not a slavish terror, but the fear a child has toward his loving and just father. **Ecclesiastes 12:13.**[38]

Q.39 *What must you remember when you are tempted?*
A. When I am tempted, I must remember that I am a new creation set free from the bondage to sin and that God always provides a way of escape. **1 Corinthians 10:13.**[39]

Q.40 *Why must you evangelize?*
A. I must evangelize because God has commanded me to do so as He delays His judgment until the full number of the elect come to faith through the proclamation of the gospel. **2 Timothy 2:10.**[40]

PART 2

On God

Q.41 *What is the Trinity?*
A. God is Trinity, which means that while there is only one God, there are three Persons in the Godhead—the Father eternally begetting, the Son eternally begotten of the Father, and the Holy Spirit eternally proceeding from the Father and the Son—and each Person is fully God, mutually indwelling each other without confusion.
Matthew 28:19.[41]

Q.42 *Who is God the Holy Spirit and what is His role?*
A. God the Holy Spirit is the third Person in the Trinity who proceeds from the Father and the Son, and who works through the Scriptures to apply salvation to the elect, equip the body of Christ, empower believers to fight sin and to follow the law of Christ, assist believers in prayer, and to keep believers in union and communion with Jesus Christ. **Galatians 5:22-23.**[42]

Q.43 *What is God's righteousness?*
A. God's righteousness is His unwavering commitment to do what is right as measured by His ultimate holiness and glory. **Romans 1:17.**[43]

Q.44 *What is the glory of God?*
A. The glory of God is the manifestation of His infinite beauty and worth, the radiance of all His perfections. **Isaiah 6:3.**[44]

Q.45 *What is God's act of creation?*
A. God's act of creation is His creating all things out of nothing by the power of His Word in the span of six days, and He declared it all very good. **Exodus 20:11.**[45]

Part 2

On the Law

Q.46 *What is the first use of the law?*
A. The first use of the law is the civil use, whereby the law restrains evil throughout society by threat of punishment. **Romans 13:3-4.**[46]

Q.47 *What is the second use of the law?*
A. The second use of the law is instructive, whereby the law shows us our own unrighteousness and inability to perfectly keep God's law and our desperate need for Christ's righteousness. **James 2:10.**[47]

Q.48 *What is the third use of the law?*
A. The third use of the law is normative, whereby, upon being set free from the curse of the law by Christ, we are able to use the law as a guide to follow, though imperfectly. **1 John 5:3.**[48]

Q.49 *What are the three types of law?*
A. The three types of law found in Scripture are civil, ceremonial, and moral. **1 Corinthians 7:19.**[49]

Q.50 *What is legalism?*
A. Legalism is the false teaching which claims that good works and the keeping of the law play a foundational role in being justified.
Galatians 5:4.[50]

Q.51 *What is antinomianism?*
A. Antinomianism is the false teaching which claims that the law has no role in a Christian's life.
John 15:10.[51]

ON JESUS CHRIST

Q.52 *What are the offices of Christ?*
A. The offices of Christ are prophet, priest, and king, whereby He teaches us, intercedes for us, and rules over us. **Hebrews 4:15.**[52]

Q.53 *What are the two estates of Christ's life?*
A. The two estates of Christ's life are His humiliation—from His birth to His burial—and His exaltation—from His resurrection through His second coming and forever. **1 Corinthians 15:3-4.**[53]

Part 2

On Salvation

Q.54 *What is meant by common grace?*
A. Common grace means that God bestows non-saving grace on believers and unbelievers alike, and that He restrains evil from its full potential in order to provide the context for redemption. **Matthew 5:45.**[54]

Q.55 *What is regeneration?*
A. Regeneration is an act of the Holy Spirit working through the Word of God to make us new creations by raising us to spiritual life and by giving us new hearts. **John 3:3.**[55]

Q.56 *What is justification?*
A. Justification is an act of God whereby our sins are pardoned and we are declared legally righteous because the righteousness of Christ has been imputed to us, which we have received by faith alone. **Romans 5:1.**[56]

Q.57 *What is adoption?*
A. Adoption is an act of God whereby He brings us into His family and gives us inheritance rights. **Galatians 4:6.**[57]

Q.58 *What is definitive sanctification?*
A. Definitive sanctification is an act of God whereby He breaks our bondage to sin, freeing us to follow righteousness. **1 Corinthians 6:11.**[58]

Q.59 *What is progressive sanctification?*
A. Progressive sanctification is a work of the Holy Spirit that conforms us increasingly into the image of Christ, in knowledge and in holiness, whereby we are able more and more to put sin to death and walk by the Spirit. **Romans 8:13.**[59]

Q.60 *What happens at death?*
A. At death the body returns to dust and the soul of the believer goes to be with Christ, while the soul of the unbeliever goes to a place of torment. **Philippians 1:23.**[60]

Q.61 *What happens at the final resurrection?*
A. At the final resurrection all the dead will be raised and their souls will be united with their bodies; believers will live with Jesus forever on the New Heavens and the New Earth, while unbelievers will be condemned to Hell for never-ending torment. **John 5:28-29.**[61]

PART 2

Q.62 *What is glorification?*
A. Glorification is the final application of redemption when Jesus will raise from the dead the bodies of all believers, unite them with their souls, and impart to them sinless, resurrection bodies like His own. **1 Corinthians 15:51-53.**[62]

Q.63 *What takes place at the final judgment?*
A. At the final judgment all persons will stand before the judgment seat of God to give an account; believers will be vindicated because they have been justified, but unbelievers will be condemned because of their unrighteousness.
2 Corinthians 5:10.[63]

ON MANKIND

Q.64 *What is marriage?*
A. Marriage is the joining together of one man and one woman to become one flesh, which was ordained by God to symbolize the relationship between Christ and His church.
Ephesians 5:31-32.[64]

ON THE CHURCH

Q.65 *What is a means of grace?*
A. A means of grace is a way God gives nourishing grace and spiritual power, through faith and by the Holy Spirit, to needy souls in the church through the preaching of the word, the ordinances, and prayer. **1 Corinthians 10:16.**[65]

Q.66 *What is the ordinance of baptism?*
A. The ordinance of baptism is an act of the church whereby a believer is immersed in water in the name of the Father, Son, and Holy Spirit, as a sign and seal of the new covenant, publicly identifying the believer with Christ's death, burial, and resurrection; and a committing of that believer to Christ and His people, to live and walk in newness of life. **Acts 2:41.**[66]

Q.67 *What is the ordinance of the Lord's Supper?*
A. The ordinance of the Lord's Supper is an act of the church whereby the believer spiritually feeds upon Christ by partaking of the bread and the wine, thereby the believer reflects upon Christ's sacrifice, receives nourishing grace, and anticipates His return. **1 Corinthians 11:23-26.**[67]

Part 2

Q.68 *What does the Bible teach regarding worship?*
A. The Bible teaches that worship is the engagement of the mind, affections, and voice in response to who God is and what He has done, and is an activity done in the Holy Spirit and according to truth as the heart delights in the awesome glory and beauty of the Triune God. **John 4:23-24.**[68]

Q.69 *What are elders?*
A. Elders are qualified men called by God to that office and recognized by the congregation to preach and teach, and to pastor and rule in the oversight of the church. **Acts 14:23.**[69]

Q.70 *What are deacons?*
A. Deacons are qualified servants called by God to that office and recognized by the congregation to care for the physical needs of church members. **Acts 6:2-3.**[70]

Internalizing the Faith

Application

Q.71 *Why must you avoid the Seductress?*
A. I must avoid the Seductress in my thoughts, with my eyes, and with my body because her enticements are a trap and her path leads to death. **Proverbs 7:10-27**[71]

Q.72 *Why is it wrong for you to be unrighteously angry?*
A. It is wrong for me to be unrighteously angry because it fills my heart with murderous intentions, ignores Christ's command to love, and is characteristic of a fool. **Proverbs 29:11.**[72]

Q.73 *How should you view money?*
A. I should view money as a gift from God but also as a possible danger; therefore, I should be generous, using my money to advance God's Kingdom on earth and to store up treasure in heaven. **Matthew 6:24.**[73]

Part 2

Q.74 *Why is it sinful for you to worry?*
A. It is sinful for me to worry because worrying reveals that I am not trusting God who sustains me and works all things for my good.
Luke 12:22-30.[74]

Q. 75 *What should the Christian do when the fear of death arises?*
A. When the fear of death arises, the Christian should remember that Jesus has freed him from the fear of death by making death a gain, because death is a spiritual resurrection that brings the Christian into the Paradise-presence of Jesus, never to die again. **Hebrews 2:14-16.**[75]

Q. 76 *What does it mean for you to forgive?*
A. To forgive means that I follow Jesus' command and example to love, that I remember how much God forgave me, that I trust God to take vengeance, that I put to death thoughts of revenge, and that I resign not to dwell on the infraction which I have forgiven. **Ephesians 4:32.**[76]

PART 3

On God

Q.77 *How do you know that God exists?*
A. I know that God exists because the Holy Spirit bears witness upon my heart and by the testimony of Scripture, the splendor of creation, and by the reality that only in God's light can I see light. **Psalm 36:9.**[77]

Q.78 *What is God's providence?*
A. God's providence is His sustaining and governing all creation, including His creatures and all their actions, according to His eternal decree, through which He has freely ordained, for His own glory, whatsoever comes to pass. **Psalm 103:19.**[78]

Q.79 *What are the two wills of God?*
A. The two wills of God are His revealed will, as set forth in Scripture, and His secret will, that which He eternally decreed. **Deuteronomy 29:29.**[79]

ON LAW AND COVENANTS

Q. 80 *What is a covenant?*
A. A covenant is a divinely initiated, oath-bound relationship, whereby God declares to His servants the blessings He will bestow, the fellowship they will have, and the curses that will befall if the covenant be broken. **Genesis 17:1-14.**[80]

Q.81 *What is the Covenant of Redemption?*
A. The Covenant of Redemption is the covenant made between the Father, the Son, and the Holy Spirit in eternity past, whereby they agreed to create and redeem a people. **Acts 4:27-28.**[81]

Q.82 *What is the Covenant of Works?*
A. The Covenant of Works, which was fulfilled by Jesus on our behalf, was originally made with Adam while he was in the estate of innocency,

whereby God held out the possibility of eternal glory conditioned upon perfect obedience.
1 Corinthians 15:44.[82]

Q.83 *What was the Old Covenant?*
A. The Old Covenant revived the conditional Covenant of Works and offered not eternal life, but the blessings of the covenant through obedience, thereby serving the New Covenant by revealing God's righteous standard and by pointing people to Christ through promises, types, and the sacrificial system. **Hebrews 8:13.**[83]

Q.84 *What is the covenant with Noah?*
A. The covenant with Noah is a common grace covenant in which God promised that He would never again flood the earth. **Genesis 9:9-11.**[84]

Q.85 *What is the covenant with Abraham?*
A. The covenant with Abraham has two dimensions: the covenant of circumcision for his physical offspring as well as a promise to save his spiritual offspring by the Messiah.
Galatians 4:22-31.[85]

Q.86 *What was the covenant with Moses?*
A. The covenant with Moses, as an outworking of the covenant of circumcision, instituted laws that governed life in Canaan, pointed to Christ, preserved His lineage, and enslaved everyone under sin. **Deuteronomy 28.**[86]

Q.87 *What is the covenant with David?*
A. The covenant with David has two dimensions: a perpetual kingdom for David's sons if they obey God, and a promise that Christ will sit on David's throne as King forever. **Psalm 132:11-12.**[87]

Q.88 *What is the Covenant of Grace?*
A. The Covenant of Grace is the unconditional New Covenant promised in the Old Testament and enacted by Christ, whereby sin is forgiven, a new heart is imparted, and a saving knowledge of God is made known to all His people. **Jeremiah 31:31-34.**[88]

Q.89 *What is the Kingdom?*
A. The Kingdom is God's reign over His redeemed people by a Messiah-King, which is visible through the church and is advanced by the Holy Spirit in the saving of sinners by the gospel. **John 18:36.**[89]

Part 3

On Jesus Christ

Q.90 *What is the active obedience of Christ?*
A. The active obedience of Christ is His obedience whereby He fulfilled for us the requirements of the law. **Romans 5:19.**[90]

Q.91 *What is the passive obedience of Christ?*
A. The passive obedience of Christ is His obedience whereby He suffered for us the penalty of our sin. **2 Corinthians 5:21**[91]

On Salvation

Q.92 *What is election?*
A. Election is an act of God that took place before the foundation of the world in which He chose some sinners for salvation according to His good pleasure alone, thereby manifesting His mercy. **Acts 13:48.**[92]

Q.93 *What is reprobation?*
A. Reprobation is God's decision made before the foundation of the world to pass over some sinners according to His good pleasure alone, leaving them subject to His justice. **1 Peter. 2:8.**[93]

Q.94 *What is the effectual call of God?*
A. The effectual call of God is a sovereign and irresistible summons by the Holy Spirit to a fellowship bond with Christ through faith. **Romans 8:30.**[94]

Q.95 *What is union with Christ?*
A. Union with Christ is a life-giving, personal, and unbreakable, Spirit-wrought faith-union, whereby we are His possession and He is our inheritance; and in this union He bestows upon us all the benefits of salvation, inseparably and simultaneously. **Colossians 3:1-4.**[95]

Q.96 *Once you are saved, can you lose your salvation?*
A. Once I am saved, I cannot lose my salvation, for the Father has me securely in His hand, Christ will finish the good work He began in me, and the Holy Spirit has sealed me. **Ephesians 1:13-14.**[96]

PART 3

ON MANKIND AND ANGELS

Q. 97 *Do believers and unbelievers think differently?*
A. While both the believer and unbeliever share the broad image of God, the unbeliever unrighteously suppresses the truth of God that is revealed to him through creation and makes himself the ultimate judge of truth; whereas the believer submits to God's Word as the ultimate foundation for knowledge and seeks to think God's thoughts after Him. **Romans 1:18-32.**[97]

Q.98 *What are limiting concepts?*
A. Limiting concepts are two God-revealed truths that appear to be irreconcilable but mysteriously require each other, interpret each other, and together advance biblical truth.
Philippians 2:12-13.[98]

Q.99 *What are angels?*
A. Angels are spiritual beings who worship and serve God by carrying out His plan and by protecting His church. **Hebrews 1:14.**[99]

Internalizing the Faith

On the Church

Q.100 *What are the keys of the Kingdom?*
A. The keys of the Kingdom are the authority held by the congregation—and exercised through the leadership of the elders—over church doctrine and church membership. **Matthew 18:15-18.**[100]

Q.101 *Why is preaching important?*
A. Preaching is important because it is God Himself speaking His Word to us through His servant, whereby we are rebuked, encouraged, matured, and conformed into the image of Christ, and all by the power of the Holy Spirit. **Hebrews 4:12.**[101]

Application

Q.102 *Why is it wrong for you to succumb to addictions?*
A. It is wrong for me to succumb to addictions because addictions are an idolatrous turning away from God's provisions, a numbing of God-given emotions, and an enslavement to something from which Christ has set me free. **John 8:34-36.**[102]

Part 3

Q.103 *How do you hold marriage in high honor?*
A. I hold marriage in high honor by fleeing from pornography, premarital sex, and adultery; and, unless I am called to singleness, by marrying a follower of Christ of the opposite sex, whom I can lavish with love. **Song 4:1-7.**[103]

Q.104 *What is the purpose of your suffering?*
A. The purpose of my suffering is to cause me to call upon God for help and to long for the return of Jesus, to test my faith, and to conform me into the image of Christ. **James 1:2-3.**[104]

Q.105 *What is spiritual warfare?*
A. Spiritual warfare is putting on the full armor of God to resist and endure attacks from the devil and his demons through prayer, fasting, and the Word of God. **Ephesians 6:10-18.**[105]

Q.106 *What must you do when melancholy sets in?*
A. When melancholy sets in, I must remember to meditate on biblical truth rather than my dark feelings and to repent of sins, idolatries, and mishandled problems that may have led to my lack of joy, trusting that God will sanctify me through this trial as I suffer with Christ.
Proverbs 17:22.[106]

Q.107 *What can you learn from the martyrs?*
A. Through the martyrs I am encouraged to endure persecution and, if necessary, to willfully lay down my life for the truth of the gospel, knowing that God's grace is sufficient for me and that Christ will avenge the blood of the martyr.
Revelation 6:9-10.[107]

ENDNOTES

[1] Num 23:19; Pss 1:2; 12:6; 119:89, 160; Prov 22:19-20; 30:5; Matt 5:17-18; Luke 16:29, 31; 24:27, 44-47; John 10:35; 17:17; Acts 17:11; Rom 15:4; 2 Tim 2:15; Titus 1:2; Heb 1:1-4; 2 Pet 1:20-21. See: John Piper, *A Peculiar Glory How the Christian Scriptures Reveal Their Complete Truthfulness* (Wheaton, IL: Crossway, 2016); Peter A. Lillback, ed., *Seeing Christ in All of Scripture: Hermeneutics at Westminster Theological Seminary* (Philadelphia, PA: WSP, 2016); John Piper, *Reading the Bible Supernaturally: Seeing and Savoring the Glory of God in Scripture* (Wheaton, IL: Crossway, 2017); Vern S. Poythress, *Reading The Word of God in the Presence of God: A Handbook for Biblical Interpretation* (Wheaton, IL:

Crossway, 2016); Lane Tipton, "The Gospel and Redemptive Historical Hermeneutics," in *Confident of Better Things: Essays Commemorating Seventy-Five Years of the Orthodox Presbyterian Church* (Willow Grove, PA: The Committee for the Historian of the Orthodox Presbyterian Church, 2011), 185-213; David Murray, *Jesus on Every Page: 10 Simple Ways to Seek and Find Christ in the Old Testament* (Nashville, TN: Thomas Nelson, 2013); Richard B. Gaffin Jr., "The Redemptive-Historical View," in *Biblical Hermeneutics: Five Views*, ed. by Stanley E. Porter and Beth M. Stovell (Downers Grove, IL: IVP, 2012), 89-110; Michael J. Kruger, *Canon Revisited: Establishing the Origins and Authority of the New Testament Books* (Wheaton, IL: Crossway, 2012); Health Lambert, *A Theology of Biblical Counseling: The Doctrinal Foundations of Counseling Ministry* (Grand Rapids, MI: Zondervan, 2016), 35-64; David B. Garner, ed., *Did God Really Say? Affirming the Truthfulness and Trustworthiness of Scripture* (Phillipsburg, NJ: P&R, 2012); L. Russ Bush and Tom J. Nettles, *Baptists and the Bible* (Nashville, TN: B&H, 1999); Cornelius Van Til, *An Introduction to Systematic Theology: Prolegomena and the Doctrines of Revelation, Scripture, and God*, ed. by William Edgar (Phillipsburg, NJ: P&R, 1974; introduction and annotations, 2007), 190-240; Vern Sheridan Poythress, *Inerrancy and the Gospels: A God-Centered Approach to the Challenges of Harmonization* (Wheaton, IL: Crossway, 2012); Herman N. Ridderbos, *Redemptive History and the New Testament Scriptures* (Phillipsburg, NJ: P&R, 1963).

² 2 Sam 23:1-2; Luke 24:49; John 14:26; Acts 1:16; 28:25-26; Rom 3:2; 1 Cor. 2:12-13; 11:23; 2 Cor 6:16; 2 Tim 3:15-17; Heb 1:1-4; 3:7. See: Peter A. Lillback and Richard B. Gaffin Jr., eds., *Thy Word is Still True: Essential Writings on the Doctrine of Scripture from the Reformation to Today* (Phillipsburg, NJ: P&R, 2013). John Calvin, *The Institutes of the Christian Religion*, ed. by John T. McNeill; trans. by Ford Lewis Battles (Louisville, KY: Westminster John Knox Press, 1960), I.7-10; Cornelius Van Til, *An Introduction to Systematic Theology: Prolegomena and the Doctrines of Revelation, Scripture, and God*, ed. by William Edgar (Phillipsburg, NJ: P&R, 1974; introduction and annotations, 2007), 241-259; B. B. Warfield, *The Inspiration and Authority of the Bible* (Phillipsburg, NJ: P&R, 1948).

³ Exod 20:4-6; 34:6-7; Num 23:19; Deut 4:15-16; 6:4; 9:7-8; 10:14; 32:4; 1 Kings 8:27; 1 Sam 15:29; Job 37:16; 41:11; Pss 24:8, 10; 27:4; 33:11; 34:8; 50:10-12; 90:2, 4; 102:25-27; 103:8; 104:24; 115:3; 139:6-10; 145:3; Isa. 45:19; 46:9-11; 55:9; 66:1-2; Jer 23:23-24; Dan 4:35; Amos 9:1-4; Mal 3:6; Matt 5:48; 6:8; 19:26; John 4:24; 17:3, 5; Acts 17:24-25, 28; Rom 16:27; 1 Cor 2:10-11; 2 Cor 1:3; Eph 1:11; Col 1:15; 1 Tim 1:11, 17; 6:15; Titus 1:2; Jas 1:17; 1 Pet 1:16; 5:10; 1 John 1:5; 3:20; 4:8; Rev 4:8, 11. See: Mark Jones, *God Is: A Devotional Guide to the Attributes of God* (Wheaton, IL: Crossway, 2017); Herman Bavinck, *Reformed Dogmatics: God and Creation*, vol. 2, ed. by John Bolt, trans. by John Vriend (Grand Rapids, MI: Baker Academic, 2004), 27-336; K. Scott Oliphint, *The Majesty of Mystery: Celebrating the Glory of an Incomprehensible God*

(Bellingham, WA: Lexham, 2016); Francis Turretin, *Institutes of Elenctic Theology*, vol. 1, ed. by James T. Dennison Jr., trans. by George Musgrave Giger (Phillipsburg, NJ: P&R, 1992), 169-252; K. Scott Oliphint, *God With Us: Divine Condescension and the Attributes of God* (Wheaton, IL: Crossway, 2012), 45-88.

[4] Gen 3:1-24; 8:21; Eccl 7:29; Ps 51:5; Mark 7:21-23; Rom 3:10-18; 8:6-9; Eph 2:1. See: J.P. Versteeg, *Adam in the New Testament: Mere Teaching Model or First Historical Man?* trans. by Richard B. Gaffin, Jr. (Phillipsburg, NJ: P&R, 2012); Mark DeVine, "Total Depravity: A Biblical and Theological Examination," in *Whomever He Wills: A Surprising Display of Sovereign Mercy*, ed. by (Cape Coral, FL: Founders Press, 2012), 16-36; John Murray, "The Imputation of Adam's Sin," in *Justified in Christ: God's Plan for us in Justification*, ed. by K. Scott Oliphint (Fearn, Ross-shire: Mentor, 2007), 205-294; John Murray, "The Fall of Man," in *Collected Writings of John Murray*, vol. 2: Systematic Theology (Carlisle, PA: Banner of Truth, 1977), 67-76; Martin Luther, *The Bondage of the Will*, trans. by J. I. Packer and O. R. Johnson (Grand Rapids, MI: Baker Academic, 1957).

[5] Deut 9:7; Josh 1:18; 1 Kings 8:46; Isa 64:6; Ps 58:3; Matt 12:31-32; John 8:34; Rom 3:23; 5:12-19; 6:23; 8:8; Heb 11:6; Jas 1:13; 1 John 1:8-10; 2:10-11; 3:4. See: John Murray, "The Nature of Sin" and "Inability," in *Collected Writings of John Murray*, vol. 2: Systematic Theology (Carlisle, PA: Banner of Truth, 1977), 77-92; Joel Beeke and Mark Jones, *A Puritan Theology: Doctrine for Life* (Grand Rapids, MI: Reformation

Heritage Books, 2012), 203-216; Geerhardus Vos, *Reformed Dogmatics*, vol. 2: Anthropology, ed. and trans. by Richard B. Gaffin Jr. (Bellingham, WA: Lexham Press, 2012-2014), 21-75; Francis Turretin, *Institutes of Elenctic Theology*, vol. 1, ed. by James T. Dennison Jr., trans. by George Musgrave Giger (Phillipsburg, NJ: P&R, 1992), 591-600.

[6] Exod 20:23; 34:14; Deut 5:7; 6:14; 2 Kings 17:35; Ps 81:9; Jer 7:9; John 14:6; Acts 4:12. See: Alistair Begg, *Pathway to Freedom: How God's Laws Guide Our Lives* (Chicago: Moody, 2003), 47-62; Timothy Keller, *Counterfeit Gods: The Empty Promises of Money, Sex, and Power, and the Only Hope that Matters* (New York: Penguin Books, 2011). G. K. Beale, *We Become What We Worship: A Biblical Theology of Idolatry* (Downers Grove, IL: IVP, 2008).

[7] Exod 32:8; 34:17; Lev 10:1-2; 19:4; 26:1; Num 3:4; Deut 4:16; 5:8; 12:30-32; 27:15; Ps 97:7; Isa 29:13; 40:18-20; Mark 7:6-7; Heb 12:28. See: Alistair Begg, *Pathway to Freedom: How God's Laws Guide Our Lives* (Chicago: Moody, 2003), 63-75; D.G. Hart and John R. Muether, *With Reverence and Awe: Returning to the Basics of Reformed Worship* (Phillipsburg, NJ: P&R, 2002); D. A. Carson, ed., *Worship by the Book* (Grand Rapids, MI: Zondervan, 2002).

[8] Lev 19:12; Deut 5:11; 6:13; Pss 8:1; 74:18; 138:2; 139:20; Prov 18:10; Jer 10:6-7; 34:16; Ezek 39:7. See: Alistair Begg, *Pathway to Freedom: How God's Laws Guide Our Lives* (Chicago: Moody, 2003), 77-96. Geerhardus Vos, *Biblical Theology: Old and New Testaments* (Carlisle, PA: Banner of Truth, 1975; reprint, 2012), 137-138.

⁹ Gen 2:2-3; Exod 20:8-11; 23:12; Isa 58:13-14; 66:23; Matt 12:11-12; 24:20; Mark 2:27-28; Luke 23:56; 1 Cor 7:19; Heb 4:9; 1 John 5:3; Rev 1:10. See: Alistair Begg, *Pathway to Freedom: How God's Laws Guide Our Lives* (Chicago: Moody, 2003), 97-114; G. K. Beale, *A New Testament Biblical Theology: The Unfolding of the Old Testament in the New* (Grand Rapids, MI: Baker Academic, 2011), 775-801; Geerhardus Vos, *Biblical Theology: Old and New Testaments* (Carlisle, PA: Banner of Truth, 1975; reprint, 2012), 138-143; Meredith G. Kline, *Kingdom Prologue: Genesis Foundation for a Covenantal Worldview* (Eugene, OR: Wipf and Stock, 2006), 33-41, 78-82; Joseph A. Pipa Jr., *The Lord's Day* (Fearn, Ross-shire: Christian Focus, 1997; reprint, 2008); Richard C. Barcellos, *Getting the Garden Right: Adam's Work and God's Rest in Light of Christ* (Cape Coral, FL: Founder Press, 2017).

¹⁰ Lev 19:3; Deut 5:16; 27:16; Prov 13:24; 20:20; 23:22; 30:11, 17; Matt 15:3-8; 19:19; Eph 6:1-3. See: Jay E. Adams, *Christian Living in the Home* (Phillipsburg, NJ: P&R, 1972); Tedd Tripp, *Shepherding a Child's Heart* (Wapwallopen, PA: Shepherd Press, 1995); Martha Peace and Stuart Scott, *The Faithful Parent: A Biblical Guide to Raising a Family* (Phillipsburg, NJ: P&R, 2010). Alistair Begg, *Pathway to Freedom: How God's Laws Guide Our Lives* (Chicago: Moody, 2003), 115-132.

¹¹ Gen 9:6; Lev 19:32; Job 31:15; Pss 22:10; 127:3-5; 139:13-16; Prov 23:22; Jer 1:5; Matt 5:21-22; 19:18; Rom 13:9; 1 Tim 5:1-2, 8; Jas 2:10-11. See: Alistair Begg, *Pathway to Freedom: How God's Laws Guide Our Lives* (Chicago: Moody, 2003), 133-151;

Notes

R. C. Sproul, *Abortion: A Rational Look at an Emotional Issue* (Orlando, FL: Reformation Trust, 2010).

[12] Deut 5:18; Prov 6:32; Matt 5:27-28; 19:18; Acts 15:29; Rom 13:9; 1 Cor 6:18; 10:8; Gal 5:19; Eph 5:3; 1 Thess 4:3-8. See: Alistair Begg, *Pathway to Freedom: How God's Laws Guide Our Lives* (Chicago: Moody, 2003), 153-169; Heath Lambert, *Finally Free: Fighting for Purity with the Power of Grace* (Grand Rapids, MI: Zondervan, 2013); Jay E. Adams, *Marriage, Divorce, and Remarriage in the Bible: A Fresh Look at What Scripture Teaches* (Grand Rapids, MI: Zondervan, 1980); Jay E. Adams, *The Christian Counselor's Manual: The Practice of Nouthetic Counseling* (Grand Rapids, MI: Zondervan, 1973), 391-412; Dave Harvey, *When Sinners Say 'I Do': Discovering the Power of the Gospel in Marriage* (Wapwallopen, PA: Shepherd Press, 2007).

[13] Lev 19:11; Deut 5:19; 1 Chron 29:11-12; Pss 24:1; 37:21; Prov 16:8; 28:24; Matt 19:18; Luke 12:15; Rom 13:9; Phil 4:12-13; 1 Tim 6:6-7; Heb 13:5; Jas 1:17. See: Alistair Begg, *Pathway to Freedom: How God's Laws Guide Our Lives* (Chicago: Moody, 2003), 171-186.

[14] Exod 23:1, 7; Lev 19:11; Deut 5:20; Ps 101:5; Prov 6:16-17; 25:18; 26:28; Matt 19:18; Luke 3:14; Rev 21:8. See: Alistair Begg, *Pathway to Freedom: How God's Laws Guide Our Lives* (Chicago: Moody, 2003), 187-203; Lou Priolo, *Deception: Letting Go of Lying* (Phillipsburg, NJ: P&R, 2008).

[15] Deut 5:21; Mic 2:1-3; Rom 7:7-10; 13:9; 1 Cor 10:5-6; Phil 4:12-13; 1 Tim 6:6-7; Jas 4:2. See: Alistair Begg, *Pathway to Freedom: How God's Laws Guide Our Lives* (Chicago:

Moody, 2003), 205-221; Thomas Watson, *The Art of Divine Contentment* (Grand Rapids, MI: Soli Deo Gloria, 2001).

[16] Matt 26:38; John 1:1-3; 2:18-22; 8:56-58; 11:27; Rom 9:5; Gal 4:4; Col 1:15-20; Heb 1:1-4; 2:17; 10:5; 2 Pet 1:1. See: Mark Jones, *Knowing Christ* (Carlisle, PA: Banner of Truth, 2015); Thomas Goodwin, *The Heart of Christ* (Carlisle, PA: Banner of Truth, 2011); Richard Bauckham, *Jesus: A Very Short Introduction* (New York: Oxford, 2011); Charles Hodge, *Systematic Theology*, vol. 2: Anthropology (Peabody, MA: Hendrickson, 2008), 378-454; Herman Bavinck, *Reformed Dogmatics: Sin and Salvation in Christ*, vol. 3, ed. by John Bolt, trans. by John Vriend (Grand Rapids, MI: Baker Academic, 2006), 233-322; John Calvin, *The Institutes of the Christian Religion*, ed. by John T. McNeill; trans. by Ford Lewis Battles (Louisville, KY: Westminster John Knox Press, 1960), II.12-14.

[17] Lev 14:6-7; 1 Sam 17. See: David Murray, *Jesus on Every Page: 10 Simple Ways to Seek and Find Christ in the Old Testament* (Nashville, TN: Thomas Nelson, 2013); Christopher J. H. Wright, *Knowing Jesus Though the Old Testament*, 2nd edition (Downers Grove, IL: IVP, 2014); Geerhardus Vos, *Biblical Theology: Old and New Testaments* (Carlisle, PA: Banner of Truth, 2012 [reprint]), 144-148; O. Palmer Robertson, *The Christ of the Prophets*, abridged edition (Phillipsburg, NJ: P&R, 2008).

[18] Gen 3:15; Isa 7:14; Matt 1:18-2:12; Luke 1:26-38; 2:1-20. See: Nancy Guthrie, ed., *Come Thou Long-Expected Jesus: Experiencing the Peace and Promise of Christmas*

(Wheaton, IL: Crossway, 2008); G.C. Berkouwer, *Studies in Dogmatics: The Work of Christ* (Grand Rapids, IL: William B. Eerdmans, 1965), 19-34; K. Scott Oliphint, *The Majesty of Mystery: Celebrating the Glory of an Incomprehensible God* (Bellingham, WA: Lexham, 2016), 80-111.

[19] Matt 3:13-27:26; Rom 5:19; 15:1-13; Gal 4:4-5; Phil 2:1-11; 1 John 3:8. See: Vern S. Poythress, *The Miracles of Jesus: How the Savior's Mighty Acts Serve as Signs of Redemption* (Wheaton, IL: Crossway, 2016); James Montgomery Boice, *The Parables of Jesus* (Chicago, IL: Moody, 1983); Herman N. Ridderbos, *The Coming of the Kingdom* (Phillipsburg, NJ: P&R, 1962); Thomas R. Schreiner, *The King in His Beauty: A Biblical Theology of the Old and New Testament* (Grand Rapids, MI: Baker Academic, 2013), 433-536; Brandon D. Crowe, *The Last Adam: A Theology of the Obedient Life of Jesus in the Gospels* (Grand Rapids, MI: Baker Academic, 2017); B. B. Warfield, "The Foresight of Jesus," in *Biblical Doctrines* (Carlisle, PA: The Banner of Truth, 1929; reprint, 2002), 71-97.

[20] Lev 14:48-53; Ps 103:12; Isa 53:5; Matt 27:32-56; Rom 5:6-11; 2 Cor 5:21; Gal 1:4; 3:13; Col 1:14, 20; 2:14; 1 Tim 2:6; Heb 9:12, 22, 25, 28; 10:12; 13:12; 1 John 1:7; 4:10; Rev 5:9. See: John Murray, *Redemption Accomplished and Applied* (Grand Rapids, MI: Eerdmans, 1955), 3-80; David Gibson and Jonathan Gibson, eds., *From Heaven He Came and Sought Her: Definite Atonement in Historical, Biblical, Theological, and Pastoral Perspectives* (Wheaton, IL: Crossway, 2013); John Calvin, *The Institutes of the Christian Religion*, ed. by

John T. McNeill (Louisville, KY: Westminster John Knox Press, 1960), II.15-17; T. Desmond Alexander, *From Paradise to the Promise Land: An Introduction to the Pentateuch* (Grand Rapids, MI: Baker Academic, 2012), 201-208, 249-259; B. B. Warfield, *Bible Doctrines* (Carlisle, PA: Banner of Truth, 1988), 327-438; J. I. Packer and Mark Dever, *In My Place Condemned He Stood: Celebrating the Glory of the Atonement* (Wheaton, IL: Crossway, 2007); Steve Jeffery, Michael Ovey, and Andrew Sach, *Pierced For Our Transgressions: Rediscovering the Glory of Penal Substitution* (Wheaton, IL: Crossway, 2007); Geerhardus Vos, *Reformed Dogmatics*, vol. 3: Christology, ed. and trans. by Richard B. Gaffin Jr. (Bellingham, WA: Lexham Press, 2014), 94-174; Herman Bavinck, *Reformed Dogmatics: Sin and Salvation in Christ*, vol. 3, ed. by John Bolt, trans. by John Vriend (Grand Rapids, MI: Baker Academic, 2006), 323-417; John W. Stott, *The Cross of Christ* (Downers Grove, IL: IVP, 1986; 2006).

[21] Ps 16:10; Isa 26:19; Dan 12:2; Luke 24:1-12; John 2:19-22; 10:18; 11:25; Acts 2:24; Rom 1:4; 4:25; 1 Cor 15:20-58; 2 Cor 3:6; 1 Tim 3:16; 1 Pet 3:18. See: Herman Bavinck, *Reformed Dogmatics: Sin and Salvation in Christ*, vol. 3, ed. by John Bolt, trans. by John Vriend (Grand Rapids, MI: Baker Academic, 2006), 430-442; Richard B. Gaffin, Jr., *Resurrection and Redemption: A Study in Paul's Soteriology* (Phillipsburg, NJ: P&R, 1987); Charles Hodge, *Systematic Theology*, vol. 2: Anthropology (Peabody, MA: Hendrickson, 2008), 626-629.

[22] Luke 24:50-51; Acts 1:9-11; Rom 8:34; Heb 7:25; 1 John 2:1. See: Herman Bavinck, *Reformed Dogmatics: Sin and Salvation in Christ*, vol. 3, ed. by John Bolt, trans. by John Vriend (Grand Rapids, MI: Baker Academic, 2006), 442-447; Charles Hodge, *Systematic Theology*, vol. 2: Anthropology (Peabody, MA: Hendrickson, 2008), 630-638.

[23] Matt 16:27; 25:31; 2 Thess 1:6-10; Titus 2:13. See: G. K. Beale and David H. Campbell, *Revelation: A Shorter Commentary* (Grand Rapids, MI: William B. Eerdmans, 2015), 399-529; Geerhardus Vos, *Redemptive History and Biblical Interpretation: The Shorter Writings of Geerhardus Vos*, ed. by Richard B. Gaffin Jr. (Phillipsburg, NJ: P&R, 1980), 415-424; B. B. Warfield, *Bible Doctrines* (Carlisle, PA: Banner of Truth, 1988), 643-664; Meredith G. Kline, *God, Heaven and Har Magedon: A Covenantal Tale of Cosmos and Telos* (Eugene, OR: Wipf and Stock, 2006), 145-207; Herman Ridderbos, *Paul: An Outline of His Theology* (Grand Rapids, MI: William B. Eerdmans, 1966), 487-562; Vern S. Poythress, *The Returning King: A Guide to the Book of Revelation* (Phillipsburg, NJ: P&R, 2000); Stanley N. Gundry and Darrell L. Bock, eds., *The Millennium and Beyond: Three Views* (Grand Rapids, MI: Zondervan, 1999); Meredith G. Kline, *Images of the Spirit* (Eugene, OR: Wipf and Stock, 1980), 97-131.

[24] Prov 3:5-6; Jer 2:13; Mark 11:22-24; 13:44; Luke 22:31-32; John 1:12; 6:35; Rom 1:5; 10:17; 12:3; 16:26; 2 Cor 5:7; Gal 5:22; Phil 1:29; 2 Thess 1:3; 1 Tim 1:13-14; Heb 11:1, 6; Jas 2:14-26; 1 Pet 1:23-2:3. See: John Murray, *Redemption Accomplished*

and Applied (Grand Rapids, MI: William B. Eerdmans, 1955), 111-122; Samuel E. Waldron, *1689 Baptist Confession of Faith: A Modern Exposition* (Grand Rapids, MI: EP Books, 2013), 223-238; Herman Bavinck, *Reformed Dogmatics: Holy Spirit, Church, and New Creation*, vol. 4, ed. by John Bolt, trans. by John Vriend (Grand Rapids, MI: Baker Academic, 2008), 96-175; Francis Turretin, *Institutes of Elenctic Theology*, vol. 2, ed. by James T. Dennison Jr., trans. by George Musgrave Giger (Phillipsburg, NJ: P&R, 1994), 558-632.

[25] Ps 51; Ezek 14:6; Matt 3:8; 4:17; Mark 1:14-15; Luke 18:13; Acts 26:20; Rom 2:4; 2 Tim 2:25; 2 Pet 3:9; Rev 2:5. See: Thomas Watson, *The Doctrine of Repentance* (Carlisle, PA: Banner of Truth, 1988); John Murray, *Redemption Accomplished and Applied* (Grand Rapids, MI: William B. Eerdmans, 1955), 111-122; Samuel E. Waldron, *1689 Baptist Confession of Faith: A Modern Exposition* (Grand Rapids, MI: EP Books, 2013), 239-252.

[26] Deut 5:29; Isa 45:22; 48:18; Ezek 18:23, 32; 33:11; Matt 22:14; 23:37; Luke 13:34; 2 Pet 3:9. See: John Murray, "The Free Offer of the Gospel," in *Collected Writings of John Murray* (Carlisle, PA: Banner of Truth, 1982), 4:113-132; John Murray, "The Atonement and The Free Offer of the Gospel," in *Collected Writings of John Murray*, vol. 1: The Claims of Truth (Carlisle, PA: Banner of Truth, 1976), 59-85; Cornelius Van Til, *Common Grace and the Gospel*, 2nd ed., ed. by K. Scott Oliphint (Phillipsburg, NJ: P&R, 2015).

[27] Pss 96:13; 98:9; Mark 1:15; Luke 18:9-14; Acts 10:42;

17:31; 24:25; Rom 3:23; 6:23; 10:9-10; 1 Cor 15:1-8. See: Greg Gilbert, *What is the Gospel?* (Wheaton, IL: Crossway, 2010).

[28] 1 Cor 9:24-27; 2 Tim 2:12; 4:7; Heb 4:11; 10:19-39; 12:1; Jas 1:12; 1 John 2:19; Rev 2:10; 3:11; 14:12. See: John Piper, *Stand: A Call for the Endurance of the Saints* (Wheaton, IL: Crossway, 2008); Thomas R. Schreiner, *Run to Win the Prize: Perseverance in the New Testament* (Wheaton, IL: Crossway, 2010).

[29] Matt 7:17-20; John 3:3, 16; 17:20-21; 20:31; Gal 5:22-23; 2 Pet 1:10; 1 John 2:29; 3:9, 14; 5:1, 4, 18. See: Martin Lloyd-Jones, *The Assurance of Our Salvation (Studies in John 17): Exploring the Depth of Jesus' Prayer for His Own* (Wheaton, IL: Crossway, 2000); R. C. Sproul, *Can I Be Sure I'm Saved?* (Orlando, FL: Reformation Trust, 2010).

[30] Gen 1:26-27; 9:6; Jas 3:8-10. See: Herman Bavinck, *Reformed Dogmatics: God and Creation*, vol. 2, ed. by John Bolt, trans. by John Vriend (Grand Rapids, MI: Baker Academic, 2004), 530-562; John Murray, "Man in the Image of God," in *Collected Writings of John Murray*, vol. 2: Systematic Theology (Carlisle, PA: Banner of Truth, 1977), 34-46; Meredith Kline, *Images of the Spirit* (Eugene, OR: Wipf and Stock, 1980).

[31] Col 3:10. See: Herman Bavinck, *Reformed Dogmatics: God and Creation*, vol. 2, ed. by John Bolt, trans. by John Vriend (Grand Rapids, MI: Baker Academic, 2004), 530-562; John Murray, "Man in the Image of God," in *Collected Writings of John Murray*, vol. 2: Systematic Theology (Carlisle, PA: Banner of Truth, 1977), 34-46; Meredith Kline,

Images of the Spirit (Eugene, OR: Wipf and Stock, 1980).

[32] Matt 16:16-20; 18:15-18; Acts 20:28; 1 Cor 1:9; 5:1-13; 12:13; Eph 2:19-22; 3:7-13; 5:22-33; 1 Tim 3:15. See: James M. Renihan, *Edification and Beauty: The Practical Ecclesiology of the English Particular Baptists, 1675-1705*, in *Studies in Baptist History and Thought* (Eugene, OR: Wipf and Stock, 2008); James M. Renihan, *Associational Churchmanship: Second London Confession of Faith, 26.12-15* (Palmdale, CA: RBAP, 2016); Pascal Denault, *The Distinctiveness of Baptist Covenant Theology: A Comparison Between Seventeenth-Century Particular Baptist and Paedobaptist Federalism*, Revised Edition (Birmingham, AL: Solid Ground Christian Books, 2017), 153; Mark Dever, *The Church: The Gospel Made Visible* (Nashville, TN: B&H, 2012); Carl R. Trueman, *Grace Alone: Salvation as a Gift of God*, ed. by Matthew Barrett (Grand Rapids, MI: Zondervan, 2017), 157-172; Kevin DeYoung and Greg Gilbert, *What is the Mission of the Church? Making Sense of Social Justice, Shalom, and the Great Commission* (Wheaton, IL: Crossway, 2011); G. K. Beale, *The Temple and the Church's Mission: A Biblical Theology of the Dwelling Place of God*, in *New Studies in Biblical Theology* (Downers Grove, IL: IVP, 2004).

[33] Ps 66:18; Prov 15:29; Matt 6:6-13; Mark 11:24; Luke 11:5-10; John 15:7; Rom 8:26; 12:12; Eph 6:18; Col 4:2; Phil 4:6; 1 Thess 5:17; 1 Tim 2:1-4; Jas 1:6-7; Rev 5:8. See: Joel Beeke and Brian G. Najapfour, eds., *Taking Hold of God: Reformed and Puritan Perspectives on Prayer* (Grand Rapids, MI: Reformation Heritage, 2011); Timothy Keller, *Prayer:*

Experiencing Awe and Intimacy with God (New York: Penguin, 2014); Arthur Bennett, ed., *Valley of Vison: A Collection of Puritan Prayers and Devotions* (Carlisle, PA: The Banner of Truth, 1975; reprinted, 2015); John Calvin, *The Institutes of the Christian Religion*, ed. by John T. McNeill; trans. by Ford Lewis Battles (Louisville, KY: Westminster John Knox Press, 1960), III.20.

[34] Ezra 8:23; Dan 9:3; 10:3; Joel 2:12; Matt 17:21; Acts 13:2; 14:23. See: John Piper, *A Hunger for God: Desiring God through Fasting and Prayer* (Wheaton, IL: Crossway, 2013); Donald S. Whitney, *Spiritual Disciplines for the Christian Life* (Colorado Springs, CO: NavPress, 1991), 159-180.

[35] 1 Chron 29:15; Ps 119:19; Prov 4:25-27; Matt 7:13-14; John 18:36; Phil 3:17-4:1; Heb 11:10-16; 13:14; Jas 4:14; 1 Pet 2:11; Rev 21:1-27. See: James J. Cassidy, "Citizens of Heaven, Strangers on Earth," in *No Uncertain Sound: Reformed Doctrine and Life* (Philadelphia, PA: Reformed Forum, 2017), 67-77; John Bunyan, *The Pilgrim's Progress* (Birmingham, AL: John L. Dagg, 2005); Jonathan Edwards, "The Pilgrim's Life," in *The Works of Jonathan Edwards*, vol. 2 (Peabody, MA: Hendrickson, 2011), 243-246; Geerhardus Vos, "Heavenly-Mindedness," in *Grace and Glory: Sermons Preaches in the Chapel of Princeton Theological Seminary* (Birmingham, AL: Solid Ground Books, 2007), 131-155; Jeremy Walker, *Passing Through: Pilgrim Life in the Wilderness* (Grand Rapids, MI: Reformation Heritage, 2015).

[36] Pss 86; 144:15; Isa 12:2; 60:21; Luke 2:10; Rom 11:36; 1

Cor 6:20; 10:31; Phil 4:4; Rev 4:11; 21:3-4. See: John Piper, *Desiring God: Meditations of a Christian Hedonist*, Revised Edition (Colorado Springs: Multnomah Books, 2011). Vern S. Poythress, *The Lordship of Christ: Serving Our Savior All of the Time, in All of Life, with All of Our Hearts* (Wheaton, IL: Crossway, 2016); Joel Beeke, *Living for God's Glory: An Introduction to Calvinism* (Orlando, FL: Reformation Trust, 2008); Martyn Lloyd-Jones, *Fellowship with God* (Wheaton, IL: Crossway, 1993).

[37] Matt 13:22; John 12:31; 14:30; 2 Cor 4:4; Eph 2:2; 1 Pet 4:2-3; 2 Pet 3:7, 10-13; Rev 21:1. See Joel Beeke, *A Loving Encouragement to Flee Worldliness* (Grand Rapids, MI: Reformation Heritage Books, 2002); C.J. Mahaney, ed., *Worldliness: Resisting the Seduction of a Fallen World* (Wheaton, IL: Crossway, 2008); Joel Beeke and Mark Jones, *A Puritan Theology: Doctrine for Life* (Grand Rapids, MI: Reformation Heritage Books, 2012), 843-858.

[38] Deut 10:12; Job 28:28; Pss 25:14; 33:8; 34:9; 86:11; 111:10; Prov 1:7; 8:13; 14:26-27; Matt 10:28; Luke 1:50; Acts 9:31; 10:35; 2 Cor 7:1. See: John Murray, *The Fear of God: The Soul of Godliness* (Birmingham, AL: Solid Ground Christian Books, 1957); Joel R. Beeke and Paul M. Smalley, *John Bunyan and the Grace of Fearing God* (Phillipsburg, NJ: P&R, 2016).

[39] Ps 119:11; Matt 4:3; 6:13; Mark 14:38; Gal 5:16; 1 Thess 3:5; Heb 4:15; Jas 1:15. See: John Owen, *Overcoming Sin and Temptation*, ed. by Kelly M. Kapic and Justin Taylor (Wheaton, IL: Crossway, 2006).

[40] Matt 24:14; 28:18-20; Mark 16:15; Luke 14:23; Acts 1:8;

Eph 4:11-12; 1 Tim 4:13; 2 Tim 4:5. See: J. I. Packer, *Evangelism and the Sovereignty of God* (Downer Groves, IL: IVP, 1961); Mark Dever, *The Gospel and Personal Evangelism* (Wheaton, IL: Crossway, 2007); Iain H. Murray, *Revival and Revivalism: The Making and Marring of American Evangelicalism 1750-1858* (Carlisle, PA: The Banner of Truth, 1994; reprint, 2009).

[41] Gen 1:26; Pss 2:7-8; 95:3, 8-9; Prov 8:22-31; Matt 3:16-17; John 10:30; Acts 5:3-4; 20:28; Rom 9:5; 15:6; 2 Cor 1:3-4; 13:14; Titus 2:13; Heb 1:5; 3:7-11; 1 Pet 1:3; 2 Pet 1:1. See: K. Scott Oliphint, *The Majesty of Mystery: Celebrating the Glory of an Incomprehensible God* (Bellingham, WA: Lexham Press, 2016), 34-53; Brandon D. Crowe and Carl R. Trueman, *The Essential Trinity: New Testament Foundations and Practical Relevance* (Phillipsburg, NJ: P&R, 2017); B. B. Warfield, *Bible Doctrines* (Carlisle, PA: Banner of Truth, 1988), 133-174; Francis Turretin, *Institutes of Elenctic Theology*, vol. 1, ed. by James T. Dennison Jr., trans. by George Musgrave Giger (Phillipsburg, NJ: P&R, 1992), 253-310; Herman Bavinck, *Reformed Dogmatics: God and Creation*, vol. 2, ed. by John Bolt, trans. by John Vriend (Grand Rapids, MI: Baker Academic, 2004), 256-336; B.A. Bosserman, *The Trinity and the Vindication of Christian Paradox: An Interpretation and Refinement of the Theological Apologetic of Cornelius Van Til* (Eugene, OR: Pickwick, 2014); Mark Jones, *God Is: A Devotional Guide to the Attributes of God* (Wheaton, IL: Crossway, 2017), 21-30; Cornelius Van Til, *An Introduction to Systematic Theology: Prolegomena and the Doctrines of*

Revelation, Scripture, and God, ed. by William Edgar (Phillipsburg, NJ: P&R, 1974; introduction and annotations, 2007), 348-368.

[42] Gen 1:2; 2:7; Ezek 37:9; Acts 2:4; Rom 8:9; 1 Cor 6:19; 12:12-27; 2 Cor 6:5-10; Eph 1:13; 1 Pet 4:7-11. See: Sinclair B. Ferguson, *Holy Spirit*, in *Contours of Christian Theology* (Downers Grove, IL: IVP, 1996); Richard B. Gaffin, Jr., *Perspectives on Pentecost: New Testament Teaching on the Gifts of the Holy Spirit* (Phillipsburg, NJ: P&R, 1979); Vern Poythress, "Modern Spiritual Gifts as Analogous to Apostolic Gifts: Affirming Extraordinary Works of the Spirit Within Cessationist Theology," in *Triperspectival Theology for the Church*, June 6, 2012 (accessed June 20, 2017), https://frame-poythress.org/modern-spiritual-gifts-as-analogous-to-apostolic-gifts-affirming-extraordinary-works-of-the-spirit-within-cessationist-theology; Geerhardus Vos, "The Eschatological Aspect of the Pauline Conception of the Spirit," in *Redemptive History and Biblical Interpretation* (Phillipsburg, NJ: P&R, 1980), 91-125; Meredith G. Kline, *God, Heaven and Har Magedon: A Covenantal Tale of Cosmos and Telos* (Eugene, OR: Wipf and Stock, 2006), 9, 13-17; Meredith Kline, *Images of the Spirit* (Eugene, OR: Wipf and Stock, 1980), 97-131.

[43] Hab 2:4; Rom 10; 2 Cor 5:21; Gal 3:11; Phil 3:9. See: John Piper, *The Future of Justification: A Response to N.T. Wright* (Wheaton, IL: Crossway, 2007), 62-71; Wayne Grudem, *Systematic Theology: An introduction to Bible Doctrine* (Grand Rapids, MI: Zondervan, 1994), 1253.

[44] Pss 19:1-14; 24:10; Isa. 42:8; Ezek. 10:4; 43:2; John 1:14; 17:1-26; Heb. 1:3; Rev. 21:23. See: John Piper, *Desiring God: Meditations of a Christian Hedonist*, Revised Edition (Colorado Springs: Multnomah Books, 2011); Meredith G. Kline, *God, Heaven and Har Magedon: A Covenantal Tale of Cosmos and Telos* (Eugene, OR: Wipf and Stock, 2006).

[45] Gen 1-2; 5; 11; Isa 43:7; Mark 10:6; Col 1:16; Rev 4:11. See: John MacArthur, *The Battle for the Beginning: Creation, Evolution, and the Bible* (Nashville, TN: Thomas Nelson, 2001); Terry Mortenson and Thane H. Ury, eds., *Coming to Grips with Genesis: Biblical Authority and the Age of the Earth* (Green Forest, AR: Master Books, 2008); Jonathan Edwards, "Dissertation on the End For Which God Created the World," in *The Works of Jonathan Edwards*, vol. 1 (Peabody, MA: Hendrickson, 2011), 94-121; David G. Hagopian, ed., *The Genesis Debate: Three Views on the Days of Creation* (Mission Viejo, CA: Crux Press, 2001).

[46] 1 Tim 2:1-2; 1 Pet 2:13-14. See: Alistair Begg, *Pathway to Freedom: How God's Laws Guide Our Lives* (Chicago: Moody, 2003), 34-37; Joel Beeke and Mark Jones, *A Puritan Theology: Doctrine for Life* (Grand Rapids, MI: Reformation Heritage Books, 2012), 556.

[47] Prov 20:9; Eccl 7:20; Ezek 18:20; Rom 3:10; 6:23; Gal 3:10, 24; 1 John 1:8. See: Alistair Begg, *Pathway to Freedom: How God's Laws Guide Our Lives* (Chicago: Moody, 2003), 37-39; Joel Beeke and Mark Jones, *A Puritan Theology: Doctrine for Life* (Grand Rapids, MI: Reformation Heritage Books, 2012), 556-557.

[48] Ps 119:44-45; John 14:15, 21, 23; 15:10; 1 Cor 9:21; Jas 2:17; 1 John 2:3; 3:4; 2 John 1:6; Rev 19:8. See: Alistair Begg, *Pathway to Freedom: How God's Laws Guide Our Lives* (Chicago: Moody, 2003), 39-44; Joel Beeke and Mark Jones, *A Puritan Theology: Doctrine for Life* (Grand Rapids, MI: Reformation Heritage Books, 2012), 557-571.

[49] Exod 20:3-17; Lev 11:1-12; 24:16. See: Philip S. Ross, *From the Finger of God: The Biblical and Theological Basis for the Threefold Division of the Law* (Fearn, Ross-shire: Mentor, 2010); Joel Beeke and Mark Jones, *A Puritan Theology: Doctrine for Life* (Grand Rapids, MI: Reformation Heritage Books, 2012), 321-334; Francis Turretin, *Institutes of Elenctic Theology*, vol. 2, ed. by James T. Dennison Jr., trans. by George Musgrave Giger (Phillipsburg, NJ: P&R, 1994), 1-168.

[50] Acts 15:1-35; Rom 3:28; Gal 5:2-6; Eph 2:8-9; 2 Tim 1:9; Titus 3:5; Jas 2:10. See: Thomas R. Schreiner, *Galatians*, in *Exegetical Commentary on the New Testament*, ed. by Clinton E. Arnold (Grand Rapids, MI: Zondervan, 2010), 155-161, 166-169, 207-219; John Murray, *The Epistle to the Romans* (Grand Rapids, MI: William B. Eerdmans, 1959; reprint, 1997), 122-126; G. K. Beale, *A New Testament Biblical Theology: The Unfolding of the Old Testament in the New* (Grand Rapids, MI: Baker Academic, 2011), 469-526.

[51] Ps 119:44-45; Matt 5:20; 7:21-23; John 14:15, 21, 23; 15:10; Jas 2:17; 1 John 2:3; 3:4, 8; 2 John 1:6; Rev 19:8. See: Mark Jones, *Antinomianism: Reformed Theology's Unwelcome Guest?* (Phillipsburg, NJ: P&R, 2013); Herman Ridderbos,

Paul: An Outline of His Theology (Grand Rapids, MI: William B. Eerdmans, 1966), 253-300; G. K. Beale, *A New Testament Biblical Theology: The Unfolding of the Old Testament in the New* (Grand Rapids, MI: Baker Academic, 2011), 835-886; Sinclair B. Ferguson, *The Whole Christ: Legalism, Antinomianism, and Gospel Assurance—Why the Marrow Controversy Still Matters* (Wheaton, IL: Crossway, 2016), 140.

[52] Isa 32:1-2; 33:22; John 1:18; 15:15; 20:31; Acts 15:14-16; 1 Cor 15:25; Heb 2:17; 7:24-25; 9:14, 28; 2 Pet 1:10-12. See: R. C. Sproul, *What Is Reformed Theology? Understanding the Basics* (Grand Rapids, MI: Baker Books, 1997), 79-98; Charles Hodge, *Systematic Theology*, vol. 2: Anthropology (Peabody, MA: Hendrickson, 2008), 462-479, 596-609; Joel Beeke and Mark Jones, *A Puritan Theology: Doctrine for Life* (Grand Rapids, MI: Reformation Heritage Books, 2012), 347-358.

[53] Luke 2:1-21; 22:47-24:53; Acts 2:32-33; Gal 4:4. See: Herman Bavinck, *Reformed Dogmatics: Sin and Salvation in Christ*, vol. 3, ed. by John Bolt, trans. by John Vriend (Grand Rapids, MI: Baker Academic, 2006), 323-484; Charles Hodge, *Systematic Theology*, vol. 2: Anthropology (Peabody, MA: Hendrickson, 2008), 610-638.

[54] Gen 20:6; 1 Sam 25:26, 34; Ps 145:9; Luke 6:35; Acts 14:17. See: John Murray, "Common Grace," in *Collected Writings of John Murray*, vol. 2: Systematic Theology (Carlisle, PA: Banner of Truth Trust, 1977), 93-122; Meredith G. Kline, *Kingdom Prologue: Genesis Foundations for a*

Covenantal Worldview (Eugene, OR: Wipf and Stock, 2006), 8-13; Cornelius Van Til, *Common Grace and the Gospel*, 2nd ed., ed. by K. Scott Oliphint (Phillipsburg, NJ: P&R, 2015).

[55] Ezek 36:26; 37:1-14; John 3:1-21; 2 Cor 5:17; Titus 3:5; 1 Pet 1:3; 1 John 2:29; 3:9; 4:7; 5:1-4. See: John Murray, *Redemption Accomplished and Applied* (Grand Rapids, MI: William B. Eerdmans, 1955), 99-110; Herman Bavinck, *Reformed Dogmatics: Holy Spirit, Church, and New Creation*, vol. 4, ed. by John Bolt, trans. by John Vriend (Grand Rapids, MI: Baker Academic, 2008), 46-59, 64-84, 87-95; G. K. Beale, *A New Testament Biblical Theology: The Unfolding of the Old Testament in the New* (Grand Rapids, MI: Baker Academic, 2011), 227-774.

[56] Rom 3:24-28; 4:6; 5:19; 8:33-34; Acts 13:38-39; 1 Cor 6:11; Gal 2:16-17; 3:8-9; 5:4-5; Phil 3:9. See: John Murray, *Redemption Accomplished and Applied* (Grand Rapids, MI: William B. Eerdmans, 1955), 123-138; Herman Bavinck, *Reformed Dogmatics: Holy Spirit, Church, and New Creation*, vol. 4, ed. by John Bolt, trans. by John Vriend (Grand Rapids, MI: Baker Academic, 2008), 176-229; John Piper, *The Future of Justification: A Response to N.T. Wright* (Wheaton, IL: Crossway, 2007); Richard B. Gaffin, Jr., "Justification and Eschatology," in *Justified in Christ: God's Plan for us in Justification*, ed. by K. Scott Oliphint (Fearn, Ross-shire: Mentor, 2007), 1-22; Lane Tipton, "Union with Christ and Justification," in *Justified in Christ: God's Plan for us in Justification*, ed. by K. Scott Oliphint (Fearn, Ross-shire: Mentor, 2007), 23-49; Herman Ridderbos, *Paul: An*

Outline of His Theology (Grand Rapids, MI: William B. Eerdmans, 1966), 159-181; G. K. Beale, *A New Testament Biblical Theology: The Unfolding of the Old Testament in the New* (Grand Rapids, MI: Baker Academic, 2011), 469-526.

[57] John 1:12; 20:17; Rom 8:14-17; Gal 3:23-26; 4:7, 28, 31; 1 Pet 3:6; 1 John 3:1-2. See: John Murray, *Redemption Accomplished and Applied* (Grand Rapids, MI: William B. Eerdmans, 1955), 139-148; Joel Beeke and Mark Jones, *A Puritan Theology: Doctrine for Life* (Grand Rapids, MI: Reformation Heritage Books, 2012), 537-554.

[58] Acts 20:32; 26:18; Rom 6:1-23; 1 Cor 1:2; 2 Thess 2:13-14; 2 Tim 2:21; 1 Pet 2:24; 1 John 3:9. See: John Murray, "Definitive Sanctification," and "The Agency in Definitive Sanctification," in *Collected Writings of John Murray*, vol. 2: Systematic Theology (Carlisle, PA: Banner of Truth, 1977), 277-293; Richard B. Gaffin, Jr., *By Faith, Not By Sight: Paul and the Order of Salvation* (Phillipsburg, NJ: P&R, 2013), 87-88.

[59] 2 Cor 7:1; Col 3:5; Phil 2:12-13; 1 Thess 5:23. See: David Powlison, *How Does Sanctification Work?* (Wheaton, IL: Crossway, 2017); John Murray, *Redemption Accomplished and Applied* (Grand Rapids, MI: William B. Eerdmans, 1955), 149-159; John Murray, "Progressive Sanctification," in *Collected Writings of John Murray*, vol. 2: Systematic Theology (Carlisle, PA: Banner of Truth, 1977), 294-304; Herman Bavinck, *Reformed Dogmatics: Holy Spirit, Church, and New Creation, vol. 4*, ed. by John Bolt, trans. by John Vriend (*Grand Rapids, MI: Baker Academic, 2008*), 230-272.

[60] Ps 116:15; Prov 14:32; Luke 16:19-30; John 12:26; 2 Cor 5:6, 8; Rev 6:9-11. See: Herman Bavinck, *Reformed Dogmatics: Holy Spirit, Church, and New Creation*, vol. 4, ed. by John Bolt, trans. by John Vriend (Grand Rapids, MI: Baker Academic, 2008), 589-643; Joel Beeke and Mark Jones, *A Puritan Theology: Doctrine for Life* (Grand Rapids, MI: Reformation Heritage Books, 2012), 819-842. Herman Ridderbos, *Paul: An Outline of His Theology* (Grand Rapids, MI: William B. Eerdmans, 1966), 487-508.

[61] Job 19:25-26; Isa 14:11; 66:24; 26:19; Dan 12:2; Matt 18:8; 24:51; 25:30, 41, 46; Mark 9:43-44, 46-48; Luke 8:31; 13:28; 14:14; John 11:24; Acts 24:15; Rom 2:7-9; 2 Thess 1:8-9; Heb 6:2, 8; 2 Pet 2:4; Jude 1:6-7, 12-13; Rev 14:9-11; 19:3; 20:4-14; 21:8. See: Meredith G. Kline, *God, Heaven, and Har Magedon: A Covenantal Tale of Cosmos and Telos* (Eugene, OR: Wipf and Stock, 2006), 145-222; Richard B. Gaffin, Jr., *Resurrection and Redemption: A Study in Paul's Soteriology* (Phillipsburg, NJ: P&R, 1987); Herman Bavinck, *Reformed Dogmatics: Holy Spirit, Church, and New Creation*, vol. 4, ed. by John Bolt, trans. by John Vriend (Grand Rapids, MI: Baker Academic, 2008), 644-730; Joel Beeke and Mark Jones, *A Puritan Theology: Doctrine for Life* (Grand Rapids, MI: Reformation Heritage Books, 2012), 819-842; Christopher W. Morgan and Robert A. Peterson, eds., *Hell Under Fire: Modern Scholarship Reinvents Eternal Punishment* (Grand Rapids, MI: Zondervan, 2007).

[62] Rom 8:19, 22-23; 1 Cor 15:20, 23, 42-45, 49-50; Phil 3:21; 1 John 3:2. See: Herman Bavinck, *Reformed Dogmatics: Holy*

Spirit, Church, and New Creation, vol. 4, ed. by John Bolt, trans. by John Vriend (Grand Rapids, MI: Baker Academic, 2008), 644-730; John Murray, *Redemption Accomplished and Applied* (Grand Rapids, MI: William B. Eerdmans, 1955), 185-193; Wayne Grudem, *Systematic Theology: An introduction to Bible Doctrine* (Grand Rapids, MI: Zondervan, 1994), 1243.

[63] Matt 12:36; 16:27; Rom 14:12; 2 Cor 5:10; Heb 9:27; 1 Pet 4:5. See: G. K. Beale, *A New Testament Biblical Theology: The Unfolding of the Old Testament in the New* (Grand Rapids, MI: Baker Academic, 2011), 469-558; Richard B. Gaffin, Jr., "Justification and Eschatology," in *Justified in Christ: God's Plan for us in Justification*, ed. by K. Scott Oliphint (Fearn, Ross-shire: Mentor, 2007), 1-22; G. K. Beale, *The Book of Revelation*, in *The New International Greek Testament Commentary* (Grand Rapids, MI: William B. Eerdmans, 1999), 934-944; Jonathan Edwards, "Sinners in the Hands of an Angry God," in *Sermons of Jonathan Edwards* (Peabody, MA: Hendrickson, 2005), 399-414.

[64] Gen 2:24; Prov 19:14; Matt 19:8-9; Mark 10:2-9; 1 Cor 7:1-40; Eph 5:22-33; 1 Pet 3:1-7. See: John Piper, *This Momentary Marriage: A Parable of Permanence* (Wheaton, IL: Crossway, 2009); Dave Harvey, *When Sinners Say 'I Do': Discovering the Power of the Gospel in Marriage* (Wapwallopen, PA: Shepherd Press, 2007).

[65] John 16:14-15; 1 Cor 10:16; Eph 5:29; Heb 4:12. See: Richard C. Barcellos, *The Lord's Supper as a Means of Grace: More Than a Memory* (Fearn, Ross-shire: Mentor, 2013);

Herman Bavinck, *Reformed Dogmatics: Holy Spirit, Church, and New Creation*, vol. 4, ed. by John Bolt, trans. by John Vriend (Grand Rapids, MI: Baker Academic, 2008), 441-495, 540-588; John Calvin, *The Institutes of the Christian Religion*, ed. by John T. McNeill; trans. by Ford Lewis Battles (Louisville, KY: Westminster John Knox Press, 1960), IV.17.

[66] Jer 31:34; Matt 3:16; John 3:23; Acts 2:38; 8:4-13, 36-39; 9:18; 10:44-48; 16:11-15, 28-34; 18:8; 19:1-7; Rom 6:3-4; Eph 4:4-6. See: Richard C. Barcellos, ed., *Recovering a Covenantal Heritage: Essays in Baptist Covenant Theology* (Palmdale, CA: RBAP, 2014); Thomas R. Schreiner and Shawn D. Wright, eds., *Believer's Baptism: Sign of the New Covenant in Christ* (Nashville, TN: B&H, 2006).

[67] Matt 26:26-29; Mark 14:17-25; Luke 22:7-21; John 13:21-30; 1 Cor 5:7; 11:23-34. See: Richard C. Barcellos, *The Lord's Supper as a Means of Grace: More Than a Memory* (Fearn, Ross-shire: Mentor, 2013).

[68] Job 1:20-21; Pss 29:2; 89:1-52; 95:1-6; 96:1-13; 100:1-5; 101:1; 146:1-2; 148:1-14; 150:1-6; Isa 12:5; Matt 4:10; Rom 12:1; Col 3:14-17; Heb 13:15; Rev 4:8, 11; 5:9-10; 11:16-18; 15:3-4; 19:10. See: Nicholas Alford, *Doxology: How Worship Works* (Conway, AR: Free Grace Press, 2017).

[69] Acts 11:30; 14:23; 15:2, 4; 20:28; 21:18; Eph 4:11; Phil 1:1; 1 Tim 2:12; 3:1-7; 5:17; Titus 1:5-9; Heb 13:17; 1 Pet 5:1-5; Jas 3:1; 5:14. See: Jeramie Rinne, *Church Elders: How to Shepherd God's People* (Wheaton, IL: Crossway, 2014); James R. White, "The Plural-Elder-Led Church," in *Perspectives on*

Church Government: 5 Views, ed. by Chad Owen Brand and R. Stanton Norman (Nashville, TN: B&H, 2004); Richard Baxter, *The Reformed Pastor* (Carlisle, PA: Banner of Truth, 1974; reprint, 2012); Martin Bucer, *Concerning the True Care of Souls*, trans. by Peter Beale (Carlisle, PA: Banner of Truth, 2009; reprint, 2016); John Piper, *Brothers, We Are Not Professionals: A Plea to Pastors for Radical Ministry* (Nashville, TN: B&H, 2002); Edmund P. Clowney, *Preaching Christ in All of Scripture* (Wheaton, IL: Crossway, 2003); G. K. Beale, *A New Testament Biblical Theology: The Unfolding of the Old Testament in the New* (Grand Rapids, MI: Baker Academic, 2011), 819-823; Andreas Köstenberger and Thomas Schreiner, *Women in the Church: An Interpretation and Application of 1 Timothy 2:9-15*, 3rd ed. (Wheaton, IL: Crossway, 2016); Thomas J. Nettles, *Living By Revealed Truth: The Life and Pastoral Theology of Charles Haddon Spurgeon* (Fearn, Ross-shire: Mentor, 2013); Ichabod Spencer, *A Pastor's Sketches: Conversations with Anxious Souls Concerning the Way of Salvation* (Pelham, AL: Solid Ground Christian Books, 2013).

[70] Acts 6:1-6; Rom 16:1; Phil 1:1; 1 Tim 3:8-13. See: David S. Apple, *Not just a Soup Kitchen: How Mercy Ministry in the Local Church Transforms Us All* (Ft. Washington, PA: CLC, 2014); Thabiti M. Anyabwile, *Finding Faithful Elders and Deacons* (Wheaton, IL: Crossway, 2012).

[71] Prov 2:16-19; 5:3-23; 6:32; 7:6-27; Acts 15:29; Rom 13:9, 13; 1 Cor 6:18; 10:8; Gal 5:19; Eph 5:3; Col 3:5; 1 Thess 4:3-8; 1 Pet 4:3. See: Heath Lambert, *Finally Free: Fighting for Purity*

with the Power of Grace (Grand Rapids, MI: Zondervan, 2013); Denny Burk, *What is the Meaning of Sex?* (Wheaton, IL: Crossway, 2013); Jay E. Adams, *The Christian Counselor's Manual: The Practice of Nouthetic Counseling* (Grand Rapids, MI: Zondervan, 1973), 391-412.

[72] Prov 14:29; 15:28; 17:27; 25:28; 29:11, 22; Eccl 7:9; Matt 5:21-22; Gal 5:19-20; Eph 4:3; Col 3:8; Jas 1:20. See: Stuart Scott, *Anger, Anxiety and Fear: A Biblical Perspective* (Bemidiji, MN: Focus Publishing, 2009); David Powlison, *Good and Angry: Redeeming Anger, Irritation, Complaining, and Bitterness* (Greensboro, NC: New Growth Press, 2017).

[73] Eccl 5:10; Matt 6:24; Luke 12:13-21; 16:9, 13; 2 Cor 9:6-7; Col 3:5; 1 Tim 6:6-10; Heb 13:5; Jas 1:17; 2:5. See: John Piper, *Desiring God: Meditations of a Christian Hedonist*, Revised Edition (Colorado Springs: Multnomah Books, 2011), 185-204; David E. Garland, *Luke*, in *Exegetical Commentary on the New Testament*, ed. by Clinton E. Arnold (Grand Rapids, MI: Zondervan, 2011), 637-655.

[74] Pss 46:2; 112:7-8; 115:11; Prov 31:25; Isa 12:2; Matt 6:31-32; John 14:1, 27; Phil 4:6; 1 Pet 3:6. See: Thomas Watson, *All Things For Good* (Carlisle, PA: Banner of Truth, 1986); Stuart Scott, *Anger, Anxiety and Fear: A Biblical Perspective* (Bemidiji, MN: Focus Publishing, 2009); Dan Wickert, "'Mary' and Paralyzing Fear," in *Counseling the Hard Cases: True Stories Illustrating the Sufficiency of God's Resources in Scripture*, ed. by Stuart Scott and Heath Lambert (Nashville, TN: B&H, 2012), 111-140; Jay E. Adams, *The Christian Counselor's Manual: The Practice of Nouthetic*

Counseling (Grand Rapids, MI: Zondervan, 1973), 413-425; Timothy Z. Witmer, *Mindscape: What to Think About Instead of Worrying* (Greensboro, NC: New Growth Press, 2014).

[75] Ps 116:15; Prov 14:32; Luke 23:43; 2 Cor 5:8; Phil 1:20-23; Rev 20:4-6. See: David Powlison, *Facing Death with Hope: Living for What Lasts* (Greensboro, NC: new Growth Press, 2008); Meredith G. Kline, *God, Heaven, and Har Magedon: A Covenantal Tale of Cosmos and Telos* (Eugene, OR: Wipf and Stock, 2006), 204-208; G. K. Beale, *Revelation: A Shorter Commentary* (Grand Rapids, MI: William B. Eerdmans, 2015), 420-451.

[76] Ps 103:10-14; Prov 10:12; 17:9; Matt 6:12-15; 18:21-22; Luke 6:37; John 13:34; Col 3:13. See: Jay E. Adams, *The Counselor's Manuel: The Practice of Nouthetic Counseling* (Grand Rapids, MI: Zondervan, 1973), 63-70, 88, 361; CCEF, "Forgiveness," https://www.ccef.org/topic/forgiveness.

[77] Prov 26:4-5; Acts 17:16-34; 2 Cor 10:3-5; 1 Pet 3:15. See: K. Scott Oliphint, *Covenantal Apologetics: Principles and Practice in Defense of Our Faith* (Wheaton, IL: Crossway, 2013); K. Scott Oliphint and Lane Tipton, eds., *Revelation and Reason: New Essays in Reformed Apologetics* (Phillipsburg, NJ: P&R, 2007); Greg L. Bahnsen, *Van Til's Apologetic: Reading and Analysis* (Phillipsburg, NJ: P&R, 1998); Thom Notaro, *Van Til and the Use of Evidence* (Phillipsburg, NJ: P&R, 1980); Jeffrey D. Johnson, *The Absurdity of Unbelief: A Worldview Apologetic of the Christian Faith* (Conway, AR: Free Grace Press, 2015).

[78] Gen 50:19-20; Exod 9:12; Pss 16:33; 135:6; 139:16; Prov 16:33; Isa 10:5-17; 46:10; Jer 32:27; Dan 4:35; John 6:37-40; Acts 4:23-31; 18:9-10; Eph 1:11; Phil 2:12-13; Heb 1:3. See: D. A. Carson, *How Long O Lord? Reflections on Suffering and Evil*, 2nd edition (Grand Rapids, MI: Baker Academic, 2006), 177-220; Herman Bavinck, *Reformed Dogmatics: God and Creation*, vol. 2, ed. by John Bolt, trans. by John Vriend (Grand Rapids, MI: Baker Academic, 2004), 337-405, 591-620.

[79] Ezek 18:23; Rom 9:22-23. See: K. Scott Oliphint, *The Majesty of Mystery: Celebrating the Glory of an Incomprehensible God* (Bellingham, WA: Lexham Press, 2016), 114-142; Herman Bavinck, *Reformed Dogmatics: God and Creation*, vol. 2, ed. by John Bolt, trans. by John Vriend (Grand Rapids, MI: Baker Academic, 2004), 240-245; Francis Turretin, *Institutes of Elenctic Theology*, vol. 1, ed. by James T. Dennison Jr., trans. by George Musgrave Giger (Phillipsburg, NJ: P&R, 1992), 218-233; Martin Luther, *The Bondage of the Will*, trans. by J. I. Packer and O. R. Johnson (Grand Rapids, MI: Baker Academic, 1957), 169-185; John Piper, *Desiring God: Meditations of a Christian Hedonist* (Colorado Springs, CO: Multnomah, 2011), 34-43; Geerhardus Vos, *Reformed Dogmatics*, vol.1: Theology Proper, trans. by Richard B. Gaffin Jr. (Bellingham, WA: Lexham Press, 2012-2014), 22-25, 92-96

[80] Gen 12, 15, 17; Jer 31. See: Richard Barcellos, ed., *Recovering a Covenantal Heritage*, 33, 475; Christ Caughery and Lee Irons, "Meredith Kline For Us: Biblical Theology,

Covenant Theology, and the Works Principle as the Foundation to the Gospel," in *Glory-Cloud Podcast*, episode 3, http://www.meredithkline.com/glory-cloud-podcast-episode-3/; Mark Jones, *Antinomianism: Reformed Theology's Unwelcome Guest?* (Phillipsburg, NJ: P&R, 2013), 49; Samuel D. Renihan, *From Shadow to Substance: The Federal Theology of the English Particular Baptists (1642-1704)* (Regent's Park College, Oxford: Centre for Baptist History and Heritage Studies, Volume 16, 2018).

[81] Matt 25:34; Luke 22:22; John 4:34; 6:37-38; 10:29; Acts 2:23-24; 4:27-28, Eph 1:4-6, 11; Col 1:16; 1 Pet 1:20-21; Rev 13:8. See: Micah and Samuel Renihan, "Reformed Baptist Covenant Theology and Biblical Theology," in *Recovering a Covenantal Heritage: Essays in Baptist Covenant Theology*, ed. by Richard C. Barcellos (Palmdale, CA: RBAP, 2014), 475-506; B. B. Warfield, *Bible Doctrines* (Carlisle, PA: Banner of Truth, 1988), 3-70; Samuel D. Renihan, *From Shadow to Substance: The Federal Theology of the English Particular Baptists (1642-1704)* (Regent's Park College, Oxford: Centre for Baptist History and Heritage Studies, Volume 16, 2018).

[82] Gen 2:15-17; Hos 6:7; Rom 5:12-19. See: Pascal Denault, *The Distinctiveness of Baptist Covenant Theology: A Comparison Between Seventeenth-Century Particular Baptist and Paedobaptist Federalism*, Revised Edition (Birmingham, AL: Solid Ground Christian Books, 2017); Nehemiah Coxe and John Owen, *Covenant Theology: From Adam to Christ*, ed. by Ronald D. Miller, James M. Renihan,

Francisco Orozco (Palmdale, CA: RBAP, 2005); Brandon D. Crowe, *The Last Adam: A Theology of the Obedient Life of Jesus in the Gospels* (Grand Rapids, MI: Baker Academic, 2017); G. K. Beale, *A New Testament Biblical Theology: The Unfolding of the Old Testament in the New* (Grand Rapids, MI: Baker Academic, 2011), 29-186; Samuel D. Renihan, *From Shadow to Substance: The Federal Theology of the English Particular Baptists (1642-1704)* (Regent's Park College, Oxford: Centre for Baptist History and Heritage Studies, Volume 16, 2018).

[83] Jer 31:32; 2 Cor 3:14; Heb 8:13; 10:11. See: Pascal Denault, *The Distinctiveness of Baptist Covenant Theology: A Comparison between Seventeenth-Century Particular Baptist and Paedobaptist Federalism*, Revised Edition (Birmingham, AL: Solid Ground Christian Books, 2017), 103-142; Samuel D. Renihan, *From Shadow to Substance: The Federal Theology of the English Particular Baptists (1642-1704)* (Regent's Park College, Oxford: Centre for Baptist History and Heritage Studies, Volume 16, 2018).

[84] Gen 9. See: Douglas Van Dorn, *Covenant Theology: A Reformed Baptist Primer* (Erie, CO: Waters of Creation, 2014), 85-88; Nehemiah Coxe and John Owen, *Covenant Theology: From Adam to Christ*, ed. by Ronald D. Miller, James M. Renihan, Francisco Orozco (Palmdale, CA: RBAP, 2005); Samuel D. Renihan, *From Shadow to Substance: The Federal Theology of the English Particular Baptists (1642-1704)* (Regent's Park College, Oxford: Centre for Baptist History and Heritage Studies, Volume 16, 2018).

NOTES

[85] Gen 12; 15; 17; 22; Acts 7:8; Gal 3:29. See: Richard C. Barcellos, ed., *Recovering a Covenantal Heritage: Essays in Baptist Covenant Theology*, (Palmdale, CA: RBAP, 2014); Jeffrey D. Johnson, *The Kingdom of God: A Baptist Expression of Covenant and Biblical Theology* (Conway, AR: FGP, 2014); Nehemiah Coxe and John Owen, *Covenant Theology: From Adam to Christ*, ed. by Ronald D. Miller, James M. Renihan, Francisco Orozco (Palmdale, CA: RBAP, 2005); Samuel D. Renihan, *From Shadow to Substance: The Federal Theology of the English Particular Baptists (1642-1704)* (Regent's Park College, Oxford: Centre for Baptist History and Heritage Studies, Volume 16, 2018);

[86] Exod 19-24; Matt 1:1-16; Luke 3:23-38; Rom 5:20; Gal 3-4. See: Richard C. Barcellos, ed., *Recovering a Covenantal Heritage: Essays in Baptist Covenant Theology*, (Palmdale, CA: RBAP, 2014), 71-108, 175-192; 257-324; Samuel D. Renihan, *From Shadow to Substance: The Federal Theology of the English Particular Baptists (1642-1704)* (Regent's Park College, Oxford: Centre for Baptist History and Heritage Studies, Volume 16, 2018).

[87] 2 Sam 7; Luke 1:32-33. See: Jeffrey D. Johnson, *The Kingdom of God: A Baptist Expression of Covenant and Biblical Theology* (Conway, AR: FGP, 2014); Douglas Van Dorn, *Covenant Theology: A Reformed Baptist Primer* (Erie, CO: Waters of Creation, 2014), 109-112; Samuel D. Renihan, *From Shadow to Substance: The Federal Theology of the English Particular Baptists (1642-1704)* (Regent's Park College, Oxford: Centre for Baptist History and Heritage

Studies, Volume 16, 2018).

[88] Gen 3:15; Jer 32:40; Matt 26:28; 2 Cor 3:6; Heb 8:6, 8, 13; 9:15; 10:16. Pascal Denault, *The Distinctiveness of Baptist Covenant Theology: A Comparison Between Seventeenth-Century Particular Baptist and Paedobaptist Federalism*, Revised Edition (Birmingham, AL: Solid Ground Christian Books, 2017); Jeffrey D. Johnson, *The Kingdom of God: A Baptist Expression of Covenant and Biblical Theology* (Conway, AR: FGP, 2014); Nehemiah Coxe and John Owen, *Covenant Theology: From Adam to Christ*, ed. by Ronald D. Miller, James M. Renihan, Francisco Orozco (Palmdale, CA: RBAP, 2005); Richard C. Barcellos, ed., *Recovering a Covenantal Heritage: Essays in Baptist Covenant Theology*, (Palmdale, CA: RBAP, 2014); Samuel D. Renihan, *From Shadow to Substance: The Federal Theology of the English Particular Baptists (1642-1704)* (Regent's Park College, Oxford: Centre for Baptist History and Heritage Studies, Volume 16, 2018).

[89] Exod 15:18; Ps 145:13; Dan 7:18; Mark 1:15; Luke 1:33; John 3:3; 1 Cor 6:9-10; 2 Thess 1:5; Rev 11:15; 21:0-14. See: Thomas R. Schreiner, *New Testament Theology: Magnifying God in Christ* (Grand Rapids, MI: Baker Academic, 2008), 41-95; Herman Ridderbos, *The Coming of the Kingdom* (Phillipsburg, NJ: P&R, 1962); Richard Bauckham, *Jesus: A Very Short Introduction* (New York: Oxford, 2011), 35-83; Micah and Samuel Renihan, "Reformed Baptist Covenant Theology and Biblical Theology," in *Recovering a Covenantal Heritage: Essays in Baptist Covenant Theology*,

ed. by Richard C. Barcellos (Palmdale, CA: RBAP, 2014), 475-506.

[90] Matt 3:15; 1 Cor 1:30; Gal 4:4-5; Phil 3:9; Heb 10:5-10. See: Brandon D. Crowe, *The Last Adam: A Theology of the Obedient Life of Jesus in the Gospels* (Grand Rapids, MI: Baker Academic, 2017); Herman Ridderbos, *Paul: An Outline of His Theology* (Grand Rapids, MI: William B. Eerdmans, 1966), 159-177; Herman Bavinck, *Reformed Dogmatics: Sin and Salvation in Christ*, vol. 3, ed. by John Bolt, trans. by John Vriend (Grand Rapids, MI: Baker Academic, 2006), 377-381; G. K. Beale, *A New Testament Biblical Theology: The Unfolding of the Old Testament in the New* (Grand Rapids, MI: Baker Academic, 2011), 470-478; Charles Hodge, *Systematic Theology*, vol. 2: Anthropology (Peabody, MA: Hendrickson, 2008), 489-526.

[91] Matt 20:28; John 1:29; Rom 3:24-25; 4:25; 5:9-10; 1 Cor 5:7; 2 Cor 5:21. See: G. K. Beale, *A New Testament Biblical Theology: The Unfolding of the Old Testament in the New* (Grand Rapids, MI: Baker Academic, 2011), 470-492; Herman Ridderbos, *Paul: An Outline of His Theology* (Grand Rapids, MI: William B. Eerdmans, 1966), 159-178; Herman Bavinck, *Reformed Dogmatics: Sin and Salvation in Christ*, vol. 3, ed. by John Bolt, trans. by John Vriend (Grand Rapids, MI: Baker Academic, 2006), 377-381; Charles Hodge, *Systematic Theology*, vol. 2: Anthropology (Peabody, MA: Hendrickson, 2008), 464-479, 610-625.

[92] Deut 7:7-8; John 8:47; 10:26; 18:37; Rom 1:7; 8:28-33; 9:6-23; Eph 1:3-6, 11; 1 Thess 1:4; 2 Thess 2:13; 2 Pet 1:10; Rev

13:8. See: John Piper, *Five Points: Towards a Deeper Experience of God's Grace* (Fearn, Ross-shire: Christian Focus, 2013), 53-62; Daniel B. Wallace, *Greek Grammar Beyond the Basics: An Exegetical Syntax of the New Testament* (Grand Rapids, MI: Zondervan, 1996), 330, 421; Greg Forster, *The Joy of Calvinism: Knowing God's Personal, Unconditional, Irresistible, Unbreakable Love* (Wheaton, IL: Crossway, 2012), 69-90; Andrew M. Davis, "Unconditional Election: A Biblical and God-Glorifying Doctrine," in *Whomever He Wills: A Surprising Display of Sovereign Mercy*, ed. by Matthew Barrett and Thomas J. Nettles (Cape Coral, FL: Founders Press, 2012), 37-76; Joel R. Beeke, *Living for God's Glory: An Introduction to Calvinism* (Orlando, FL: Reformation Trust, 2008), 60-73; Wayne Grudem, *Systematic Theology: An introduction to Bible Doctrine* (Grand Rapids, MI: Zondervan, 1994), 1241; B. B. Warfield, "Predestination," in *Biblical Doctrines* (Carlisle, PA: The Banner of Truth, 1988; reprint, 2002), 3-70; John Murray, *The Epistle to the Romans* (Grand Rapids, MI: William B. Eerdmans, 1968; paperback edition, 1997), I:315-321, II:1-45; John Piper, *The Justification of God: An Exegetical and Theological Study of Romans 9:1-23*, 2nd edition (Grand Rapids, MI: Baker, 1993); Thomas R. Schreiner, *Romans*, in *Baker Exegetical Commentary on the New Testament* (Grand Rapids, MI: Baker, 1998), 448-455, 476-549; Loraine Boettner, *The Reformed Doctrine of Predestination* (Phillipsburg, NJ: P&R, 1932); Robert A. Peterson and Michael D. Williams, *Why I Am Not An Arminian* (Downers

Grove, IL: IVP Books, 2004), 42-66; John Calvin, *The Institutes of the Christian Religion*, ed. by John T. McNeill; trans. by Ford Lewis Battles (Louisville, KY: Westminster John Knox Press, 1960), III.2.11-12; III.21-24; Isaac Backus, *The Doctrine of Sovereign Grace: Open and Vindicated from Holy Scripture* (Birmingham, AL: Solid Ground Christian Books, 2009).

[93] Prov 16:4; Matt 13:10-15; John 8:44; 10:26; 12:39-40; Rom 9:14-24; 2 Thess 2:11; Jude 1:4. See: Joel R. Beeke, *Living for God's Glory: An Introduction to Calvinism* (Orlando, FL: Reformation Trust, 2008), 11, 66; Daniel B. Wallace, *Greek Grammar Beyond the Basics: An Exegetical Syntax of the New Testament* (Grand Rapids, MI: Zondervan, 1996), 101, 417-418; Loraine Boettner, *The Reformed Doctrine of Predestination* (Phillipsburg, NJ: P&R, 1932), 104-126; Cornelius Van Til, *Common Grace and the Gospel*, 2nd ed., ed. by K. Scott Oliphint (Phillipsburg, NJ: P&R, 2015), 145-168; Wayne Grudem, *Systematic Theology: An introduction to Bible Doctrine* (Grand Rapids, MI: Zondervan, 1994), 1253.

[94] John 6:44; Acts 2:39; 16:14; 26:17-18; Rom 11:7; 1 Cor 1:9, 23-24; 4:1; 2 Thess 2:13-14; 2 Tim 1:8-9; 2 Pet 1:10. See: John Murray, *Redemption Accomplished and Applied* (Grand Rapids, MI: William B. Eerdmans, 1955), 91-98; John Piper, *Five Points: Towards a Deeper Experience of God's Grace* (Fearn, Ross-shire: Christian Focus, 2013), 25-36; Joel R. Beeke, *Living for God's Glory: An Introduction to Calvinism* (Orlando, FL: Reformation Trust, 2008), 101-114; Robert A Peterson and Michael D. Williams, *Why I Am Not an*

Arminian (Downers Grove, IL: IVP Books, 2004), 173-191.

[95] Deut 33:27; Ps 73:25; Lam 3:24; Mal 3:17; John 14:1-3; 15:4; 16:14-15; Rom 5:12-19; 6:2-11; 8:1, 9-10; 1 Cor 15:22; 2 Cor 5:17; Gal 2:20; Eph 1:3-7, 13-14; 2: 4-6; 3:16-17; Col 2:6; 1 Tim 3:16; 1 John 1:3. See: John Murray, *Redemption Accomplished and Applied* (Grand Rapids, MI: William B. Eerdmans, 1955), 171-184; Jeffrey C. Waddington, "Union with Christ and the *Ordo Salutis*," in *No Uncertain Sound: Reformed Doctrine and Life* (Philadelphia, PA: Reformed Forum, 2017), 32-50; Richard B. Gaffin, Jr., *By Faith, Not By Sight: Paul and the Order of Salvation* (Phillipsburg, NJ: P&R, 2013); Sinclair B. Ferguson, *Holy Spirit*, in *Contours of Christian Theology* (Downers Grove, IL: IVP, 1996).

[96] Jer 32:40; Matt 13:20-22; Mark 13:13; Luke 8:9-14; John 10:27-30; Rom 8:30; 1 Cor 1:8-9; 15:1-2; Col 1:21-23; Phil 1:6; 3:12; 1 Thess 5:23-24; 2 Tim 2:10-12; Heb 3:12-13; 12:15-17; 13:20-21; 1 Pet 1:5; 2 Pet 1:3-11; 1 John 2:19; Jude 24-25; Rev 2:7. See: Thomas R. Schreiner, *Run to Win the Prize: Perseverance in the New Testament* (Wheaton, IL: Crossway, 2010); Daniel B. Wallace, *Greek Grammar Beyond the Basics: An Exegetical Syntax of the New Testament* (Grand Rapids, MI: Zondervan, 1996), 330, 458-459, 468, 474, 564, 568, 632; Greg Forster, *The Joy of Calvinism: Knowing God's Personal, Unconditional, Irresistible, Unbreakable Love* (Wheaton, IL: Crossway, 2012), 121-144; John Piper, *Five Points: Towards a Deeper Experience of God's Grace* (Fearn, Ross-shire: Christian Focus, 2013), 63-76.

[97] Gen 3:1-7; 2 Cor 4:4; 11:3; Eph 2:1; Col 2:13; 2 Tim 4:2-4.

See: Greg L. Bahnsen, *Presuppositional Apologetics: Stated and Defended* (Nacogdoches, TX: Covenant Media, 2008), 77-136; Greg L. Bahnsen, *Van Til's Apologetic: Reading and Analysis* (Phillipsburg, NJ: P&R, 1998), 144-460; William D. Dennison, *In Defense of the Eschaton: Essays in Reformed Apologetics,* ed. by James Douglas Baird (Eugene, OR: Wipf & Stock, 2015), 3-35, 105-154; James Douglas Baird, "Analogical Knowledge: A Systematic Interpretation of Cornelius Van Til's Theological Epistemology," *Mid-America Journal of Theology* 26 (2015): 77-103; Cornelius Van Til, *A Christian Theory of Knowledge* (Phillipsburg, NJ: P&R, 1969); K. Scott Oliphint and Lane Tipton, eds., *Revelation and Reason: New Essays in Reformed Apologetics* (Phillipsburg, NJ: P&R, 2007), 59-73; K. Scott Oliphint, *Thomas Aquinas* (Phillipsburg, NJ: P&R, 2017).

[98] Hab 1:6, 11; Matt 11:25-30; Acts 2:23; 4:27-28. See: Cornelius Van Til, *Common Grace and the Gospel*, 2nd ed., ed. by K. Scott Oliphint (Phillipsburg, NJ: P&R, 2015), vii-19; B.A. Bosserman, *The Trinity and the Vindication of Christian Paradox: An Interpretation and Refinement of the Theological Apologetic of Cornelius Van Til* (Eugene, OR: Pickwick, 2014); K. Scott Oliphint, *The Majesty of Mystery: Celebrating the Glory of an Incomprehensible God* (Bellingham, WA: Lexham Press, 2016).

[99] Exod 23:20; Pss 34:7; 91:11; 103:20; 148:2; Zech 1:10-11; Matt 13:41; 18:10; 22:30; 24:31; Luke 1:26-38; 15:10; Acts 7:30, 35, 38, 53; 8:26; Col 1:16; 1 Tim 5:21; Heb 13:2; Jude 1:6, 9; Rev 12:7; 19:10. See: R. C. Sproul, *Unseen Realities: Heaven, Hell,*

Angels, and Demons (Fearn, Ross-shire: Christian Focus, 2011); Herman Bavinck, *Reformed Dogmatics: God and Creation*, vol. 2, ed. by John Bolt, trans. by John Vriend (Grand Rapids, MI: Baker Academic, 2004), 443-472.

[100] Matt 16:19; 18:15-20; 1 Cor 5; 2 Cor 2:6-7; Gal 1:6-9. See: Jonathan Leeman, *Political Church: The Local Assembly as Embassy of Christ's Rule* (Downers Grove: IVP Academic, 2016); Jonathan Leeman, *Church Membership: How the World Knows Who Represents Jesus* (Wheaton, IL: Crossway, 2012); Mark Dever, *The Church: The Gospel Made Visible* (Nashville, TN: B&H, 2012).

[101] Neh 8:8; Mark 16:15; Rom 10:14; 1 Cor 1:21, 23; 1 Tim 4:13; 2 Tim 2:15; 3:16; 4:2-4; 1 Pet 4:11. See: Don Kistler, ed., *Feed My Sheep: A Passionate Plea for Preaching*, 2nd ed. (Orlando, FL: Reformation Trust, 2002); David R. Helm, *Expository Preaching: How We Speak God's Word Today* (Wheaton, IL: Crossway, 2014); Edmund P. Clowney, *Preaching Christ in All of Scripture* (Wheaton, IL: Crossway, 2003).

[102] Prov 23:29-35; John 8:34-36; Rom 6:16-18; 13:13; 1 Cor 6:10; Gal 5:21; Eph 5:8-18; 1 Pet 4:3; 5:8. See: Edward T. Welch, "Addictions: New Ways of Seeing, New Ways of Walking Free," in *The Journal of Biblical Counseling*, Volume 19, Number 3 (CCEF, Spring 2001); Edward T. Welch, *Blame it on the Brain? Distinguishing Chemical Imbalances, Brain Disorders, and Disobedience* (Phillipsburg, NJ: P&R, 1998), 183-202; Edward T. Welch, *Addictions: A Banquet in the Grave: Finding Hope in the Power of the Gospel* (Phillipsburg, NJ: P&R, 2001); Jay E. Adams, *The Christian Counselor's Manual: The Practice of Nouthetic Counseling* (Grand Rapids, MI: Zondervan, 1973), 161-216.

[103] Gen 2:24; Lev 18:20, 22; Matt 19:8-9; Mark 10:2-9; Rom 1:26-28; 1 Cor 6:9; Gal 5:19; 1 Tim 1:9-11; Heb 12:16; 13:4; Jude 1:7. See: Dave Harvey, *When Sinners Say 'I Do': Discovering the Power of the Gospel in Marriage* (Wapwallopen, PA: Shepherd Press, 2007); Heath Lambert, *Finally Free: Fighting for Purity with the Power of Grace* (Grand Rapids, MI: Zondervan, 2013); Denny Burk, *What is the Meaning of Sex?* (Wheaton, IL: Crossway, 2013); Iain M. Duguid, *The Song of Songs, Tyndale Old Testament Commentaries* (Downers Grove, IL: IVP, 2015). Sam Allberry, *Is God Anti-Gay? And Other Questions About Homosexuality, the Bible and Same-Sex Attraction* (Purcellville, VA: The Good Book Company, 2013); Laura Hendrickson, "'Mariana' and Surviving Sexual Abuse," in *Counseling the Hard Cases: True Stories Illustrating the Sufficiency of God's Resources in*

Scripture, ed. by Stuart Scott and Heath Lambert (Nashville, TN: B&H, 2012), 25-56; Kevin Carson, "'Jason' and Homosexuality," in *Counseling the Hard Cases: True Stories Illustrating the Sufficiency of God's Resources in Scripture*, ed. by Stuart Scott and Heath Lambert (Nashville, TN: B&H, 2012), 227-256; Edward T.. Welch, *Blame It on the Brain? Distinguishing Chemical Imbalances, Brain Disorders, and Disobedience* (Phillipsburg, NJ: P&R, 1998), 151-182.

[104] Deut 32:39; Job 1:20-22; 2:10; 42:11; Pss 23:4; 116:15; Isa 45:7; Lam 3:37-38; Amos 3:6; Luke 9:23; 21:28; John 9:3; Acts 5:41; Rom 5:3-4; 8:18, 28; 1 Cor 15:55; 2 Cor 4:16-17; Phil 1:21, 29; 1 Thess 4:13; Heb 12:7; Jas 1:2-3; 1 Pet 4:16, 19; 5:10; Rev 21:3-4. See: D. A. Carson, *How Long O Lord? Reflections on Suffering and Evil*, 2nd edition (Grand Rapids, MI: Baker Academic, 2006); John Piper and Justin Taylor, eds., *Suffering and the Sovereignty of God* (Wheaton, IL: Crossway, 2006); Christopher W. Morgan and Robert A. Peterson, eds., *Suffering and the Goodness of God*, in *Theology in Community* (Wheaton, IL: Crossway, 2008); Brian H. Cosby, *Suffering and Sovereignty: John Flavel and the Puritans on Afflictive Providence* (Grand Rapids, MI: Reformation Heritage Books, 2012); Timothy Keller, *Walking With God Through Pain and Suffering* (New York: Penguin Books, 2013); Heath Lambert, *A Theology of Biblical Counseling: The Doctrinal Foundations of Counseling Ministry* (Grand Rapids, MI: Zondervan, 2016), 247-273.

[105] John 8:44; 2 Cor 11:14-15; 2 Thess 2:9; 1 Pet 5:8-9; Rev 20:2. See: Joel R. Beeke, *Fighting Satan: Knowing His Weaknesses, Strategies, and Defeat* (Grand Rapids, MI: Reformation Heritage Books, 2015); Joel R. Beeke and Mark Jones, *A Puritan Theology: Doctrine for Life* (Grand Rapids, MI: Reformation Heritage Books, 2012), 189-202; Bodie Hodge, *The Fall of Satan: Rebels in the Garden* (Green Forest, AR: Master Books, 2011).

[106] Ps 37:4; Prov 12:25; 2 Cor 7:10; Phil 4:4; 1 Thess 5:16-18. See: Edward T. Welch, *Depression: Looking Up from the Stubborn Darkness* (Greensboro, NC: New Growth Press, 2011); Edward T. Welch, *Depression: The Way Up When You Are Down* (Phillipsburg, NJ: P&R, 2000); Edward T. Welch, *Blame It on the Brain? Distinguishing Chemical Imbalances, Brain Disorders, and Disobedience* (Phillipsburg, NJ: P&R, 1998), 115-130; Jay Adams, *Competent to Counsel: Introduction to Nouthetic Counseling* (Grand Rapids, MI: Zondervan, 1970), 105-127; Health Lambert, "'Sarah' and Postpartum Depression," in *Counseling the Hard Cases: True Stories Illustrating the Sufficiency of God's Resources in Scripture*, ed. by Stuart Scott and Heath Lambert (Nashville, TN: B&H, 2012), 85-110; David Powlison, *Seeing With New Eyes: Counseling and the Human Condition Though the Lens of Scripture* (Phillipsburg, NJ: P&R, 2003), 211-224.

[107] Matt 10:28-33; Heb 11:35; 1 Pet 4:14-16; Rev 13:7-10. See: *Fox's Book of Martyrs*, http://www.ccel.org/f/foxe/martyrs/home.html; Ruth A. Tucker, *From Jerusalem to Irian Jaya: A*

Biographical History of Christian Missions (Grand Rapids, MI: Zondervan, 2004); John Piper, *Desiring God: Meditations of a Christian Hedonist* (Colorado Springs, CO: Multnomah, 2011), 253-288.

Notes

Internalizing the Faith